MANAGING PUBL
ACCESS COMPUTE

A How-To-Do-It Manual for Librarians

Donald A. Barclay

*HOW-TO-DO-IT MANUALS
FOR LIBRARIANS*

NUMBER 96

NEAL-SCHUMAN PUBLISHERS, INC.
New York, London

Published by Neal-Schuman Publishers, Inc.
100 Varick Street
New York, NY 10013

The paper used in this publication meets the minimum requirements of American National Standard for Information Sciences—Permanence of Paper for Printed Library Materials, ANSI Z39.48–1992. ∞

Printed and bound in the United States of America.

ISBN 1–55570–361–5

CONTENTS

LIST OF FIGURES

ACKNOWLEDGMENTS

It takes a lot of help to write a book like this. First off, there are two groups I would like to acknowledge. One is the members of the Web4Lib electronic discussion group (Roy Tennant, list owner); they are a never-ending source of good information and sound advice. The other group is InFoPeople (especially Carole Leita), providers of a truly informative Website and gracious granters of permission to quote from it. Huge thank yous are also due to Clarence Witson (Houston Academy of Medicine—Texas Medical Center Library) and Pamela Talene Hale (University of Houston Library), a pair of dear colleagues who waded through early drafts and offered suggestions that kept me from wandering onto the path to folly. I also owe a debt of gratitude to Charles Harmon, the most patient and encouraging editor any writer could want. Finally, I thank my wife, Darcie Reimann Barclay, for more than tolerating all those evenings and weekends I spent planted in front of our home computer. I thank her, too, for her expert advice, contributions, and assistance. I could not have written this book without her.

PREFACE

This book was not written by a systems expert. I started out as a reference librarian, but, because I entered the profession just as the electronic Big Bang was changing libraries forever, I ended up learning a lot more about computers than I ever thought I would. In time, I found myself—a public-service librarian by inclination—not just working with, but actually managing, public-access computers. As someone with one foot in the world of traditional public service and the other in the world of computers, it has long seemed to me that too many books about computers in libraries fly off into the technosphere without concerning themselves with such down-to-earth issues as what to do when user demand for public-access workstations outstrips supply or how to keep a staff of part-time lab assistants up-to-date in their training. Even when it is technical information that librarians who work with public-access computers seek, a lot of the information out there is irrelevant—searching the Web for a topic such as "Computer Security" pulls up thousands of hits dealing with network firewalls and Web page break-ins, but produces almost nothing on how to keep a sixth grader from replacing the default Windows wallpaper with supermodel photographs.

Though this book necessarily concerns itself with computer technology, it approaches technology as a tool for providing public-service, not as an end in itself. Along the same lines, the overarching purpose here is to help librarians, and others, effectively manage public-access computers so as to further the missions of their institutions—not to turn anyone into a systems expert.

If experience has taught me anything, it is that effective management of public-access computers is a balancing act. On one end of the see-saw there is the need to provide the public with equitable access to computers, while on the other end there is the need to provide for the security and maintenance of those same computers and their software. Achieving such a balance calls for knowledge of technology, of course, but it also demands sound public-service practices and effective staff management. It is my hope that readers of this book will come away with an appreciation for the art of managing public-access computers, as well as an understanding of how the intersection of technology, public service, and staff management all contribute to a successful public-access computer operation.

The intended audience for this book is front-line to upper-level managers who need to make critical decisions about public-access computers in libraries and other institutions. This book should also prove useful to non-managerial public-service staff who assist library patrons with computers on a day-to-day basis, as well as to computer professionals who are interested in expanding their understanding of the public-service side of public-access computers. While this book assumes some knowledge of microcomputer technology on the part of the reader, it does not assume that readers are systems librarians, computer professionals, or otherwise members of the technological elite.

This book is organized to progress from more technological to more managerial topics. The first chapter—which answers the question, "What Does a Manager Need to Know About Technology?"—is followed by chapters which tackle such topics as facilities planning and management, computer hardware and software, CD-ROM and DVD, printing, and system security. Recognizing that managers of public-access computers rarely operate in a vacuum, Chapter 7 concerns itself with the art of working with systems department staff. Two later chapters focus on managing, training, and communicating with public-access computer staff, while the final chapter covers working with computer users.

Included throughout this book are citations to a number of online information resources. Most of these resources are pages on Websites that contain more useful information than I could ever hope to cite. I encourage readers to explore these Websites in depth, not just the pages to which I have pointed.

INTRODUCTION: A PUBLIC-SERVICE APPROACH TO PUBLIC-ACCESS COMPUTERS

Imagine how odd it would seem if someone walked into a historical museum, stepped over the velvet rope, and plopped down onto a three-hundred-year-old chair. Or if that same museum visitor asked to take home (for two weeks) a uniform from the World War I exhibit. Odd indeed. Yet it is considered perfectly reasonable for library patrons to pore over seventeenth-century books in special-collections rooms or to take home early twentieth-century (and older) books by the armful. This speaks both to the unique services provided by libraries as well as to the durability of that technological marvel we call *the book*.

Similarly, while no rational member of the general public would walk into a place of business, a government office, or a school building expecting free and unfettered access to a computer, the general public increasingly expects libraries to provide free access to computers; in particular, access to computers connected to that technological marvel we call *the Internet*. Perhaps the public expects to access computers in libraries because of the long association between libraries and free access to information. Perhaps it is because library public-access online catalogs have been around for so long, and have become so common, that the habit of using computers in libraries is ingrained in the public mind. Whatever the source of the public's expectations for computer access in libraries, meeting such expectations raises a number of management questions for libraries; the most basic of which is, "Should libraries provide public-access computers?"

For anyone who would pick up this book, the answer to the above question may seem obvious, but it is nevertheless a question worth contemplating if for no other reason than the fact that anything *obvious* should always be questioned.

In the 1960s, library journals began publishing more and more articles about "mechanized information systems," most of which were conceived of as tools for performing technical-service functions such as generating paper cards to be filed in the drawers of the then-ubiquitous card catalog (itself a technological marvel). Though, in the early days of the computerization debate, more than a few librarians questioned the whole idea of computers in

---

Focus On:

Beware the Obvious

Should we allow users to play games on library computers?
Obviously not!

Should users have to pay to print from library computers?
Obviously yes!

Any time the solution to a problem seems completely obvious, an alarm bell should go off in the managerial brain. Is the solution *really* so obvious? Is the obvious course of action the only option? Is my certainty on this matter the result of good thinking, or have I focused on some petty point while ignoring a much larger issue? What might I have overlooked here?

When answers seem obvious, it is crucial to seek out "fresh eyes"—some person or (ideally) persons who can look at the situation from a different perspective than you and those immediately around you. You might find fresh eyes in another department within your library or in a library across town. Posting to a listserv is a good way to solicit the opinions of those who see things differently, as is talking—and listening—to those outside of the library field.

In the end, the obvious solution or course of action may turn out to be the right one, but it is good managerial practice to question the obvious rather than accept it without pause. This is especially true when it comes to working with computers, a field so fast-changing that what was obvious only a few weeks ago may not be obvious today.

---

libraries, librarian resistance to computers all but vanished from the professional literature as the price of computing power plunged and the role of library computers spread from behind-the-scenes applications to public-access online catalogs, CD-ROM workstations, and networked computers. Some outside the library profession, however, still continue to openly question the computerization of libraries, as is evidenced by Nicholson Baker's controversial 1994 *New Yorker* article "Discards"[1] and Clifford Stoll's equally controversial 1995 *Silicon Snake Oil*[2]—a book which argues, in part, that libraries should spend their money on print materials, not computers. While the library literature will never again see anything as flamboyantly anti-computer as Mason Ellsworth's 1971 *College & Research Libraries* article "The Great Gas Bubble Prick't or, Computers Revealed-by a Gentleman of Quality,"[3] there are still those in the profession who question, with good reason, whether libraries have given up too much of their heart and soul in the rush to provide computer access.

The arguments against public-access computers in libraries are legitimate and worthy of serious consideration:

- Public-access computers are a cost center, with the funds to pay for, maintain, and perpetually upgrade computers often coming from the budgets of other library services and materials.
- Libraries are misguided to spend money providing people with the same kind of computer resources they have in their homes, businesses, and schools. Instead, libraries should spend money on the things that most people do not have in their homes, business, and schools; namely, large and varied collections of print books and periodicals.
- Computers actually alienate some library users because they are noisy, take up valuable space, are often aesthetically unappealing, and demand frequent attention from library staff who could otherwise be assisting library users.
- Attaching public-access computers to the Internet opens up libraries to whole new worlds of hassles associated with pornography, sexual harassment, parental rights, copyright, privacy, accessibility, and free-speech.

On the other hand, the arguments in favor of placing public-access computers in libraries, however familiar, are compelling:

- Public-access computers open up a whole world of information—much of it available free of charge—to library users and the librarians who serve them.
- The electronic networking of information resources, such as databases and online journals, can result in cost savings for libraries, and public-access computers are necessary to make such networked resources available to end users.

- Library public-access computers allow those who do not have access to home or business computers the opportunity to participate in the electronic information society.
- Libraries that fail to become part of the electronic information revolution are in danger of being seen as unnecessary, outdated book museums.
- The library-using public overwhelmingly wants computer access to information.

However the arguments stack up, it is clear that those in favor of public-access computers are winning the battle for the hearts, minds, and dollars of libraries. In 1998, 85.8 percent of U.S. public libraries (urban, suburban, and rural) were connected to the Internet, and of these, 88.5 percent provided public-access to the Internet.[4] Public-access computers, like it or not, are now as much a part of the library landscape as the book and the magazine. The computer advocates have won the revolution; now it is up to library managers to do the tough day-to-day job of turning the revolution into a workaday reality.

From a public-service perspective, public-access computers present libraries with a whole range of complex questions, some of which include:

- How many computers do we need and how will we make space for them?
- What kind of hardware and software should we acquire and how will we pay for it?
- How do we protect computer hardware and software from theft or harm?
- What kinds of computer services should we provide:
  - Online catalog?
  - Databases?
  - Internet?
  - Word processing?
  - Spreadsheets and other productivity software?
- Should certain classes of users (such as adults, cardholders, faculty members) have more computer privileges than other classes of users (such as children, non-cardholders, undergraduates)?
- Should we prohibit certain computer activities? If so, which ones?
  - E-mail?
  - Chat?
  - Viewing pornography?

- Game playing?
- Internet gambling?
- What are the legal ramifications of having public-access computers in libraries?
- What level of end-user training and/or one-on-one help do we provide?
- Who among the library staff will provide such training and help?
- How do we keep library staff trained and up-to-date when change is a constant?

While the above questions are complex, experienced public-service librarians will recognize that the public-service issues they touch upon are no different from the public-service issues with which libraries have always dealt. All are questions that come down to the old and familiar problem of how to manage scarce resources so as to provide the most good for the most people. And, while the increasing importance of computers in libraries demands flexibility in the way we manage libraries, it does not mean discarding the wealth of public-service knowledge the profession has accumulated through years of practice and research. Even in those cases where computers present problems that seem unlike any that librarians have dealt with in the past, finding analogies in libraries' long-established traditions of respectful public-service and commitment to the ideal that information is for everyone can lead to workable, even elegant, solutions.

NOTES

1. Baker, Nicholson. 1994. "Annals of Scholarship: Discards." *New Yorker*. 7 (April 4):64-86.
2. Stoll, Clifford. 1995. *Silicon Snake Oil: Second Thoughts on the Information Highway*. New York: Doubleday.
3. Mason, Ellsworth. 1971. "The Great Gas Bubble Prick't or, Computers Revealed-by a Gentleman of Quality." *College and Research Libraries*. 3 (May):183–196.
4. Bertot, John Carlo and Charles R. McClure. 1998. *The 1998 National Survey of U.S. Public Library Outlet Internet Connectivity: Final Report*. Washington, DC: National Commission on Libraries and Information Science.

1 WHAT DOES A MANAGER NEED TO KNOW ABOUT TECHNOLOGY?

What does a manager of public-access computers need to know about software, hardware, networking, and all the other technology that makes computers compute? The short answer is, "The more, the better." In the ideal case, a manager would have all the knowledge of a computer professional coupled with all the knowledge of an experienced public-service librarian. In actual practice, persons completely expert in both areas are rare—if they exist at all. Most successful managers possess, instead, some happy mixture of technical and public-service knowledge.

How much and what kind of technical knowledge a manager must have depends a great deal on the amount and quality of systems support the manager has, as well as on the technical knowledge of the public-service staff who work with the manager. If you have top-notch systems support, or if you are fortunate enough to be surrounded by a public-service staff full of computer whizzes, you can get by with a lot less computer knowledge than if everyone looks to you as the computer guru. This chapter discusses, in a general way, the kinds of technological knowledge a manager should have. It also explains, in the plainest English possible, some selected technological concepts with which managers will want to have at least some familiarity.

KINDS OF KNOWLEDGE: MICRO-LEVEL AND MACRO-LEVEL

One kind of technological knowledge a manager should have is micro-level knowledge; that is, the kind of detailed, committed-to-memory knowledge that is necessary to carry out common computer tasks. Typical examples of micro-level knowledge include:

- Hitting the Ctrl-Alt-Del keys simultaneously to reboot a frozen computer.
- Pressing F1 to see a help screen.
- Clicking the Start button to access programs in Windows 95.
- Deleting the Microsoft Word normal.dot file to remove (yet again) the "Have A Nice Day" virus from an infected computer.

1

The type of micro-level knowledge described above is transferable from place to place and from application to application. Once you acquire such micro-level knowledge (usually through some combination of experience, help screens, manuals, or formal training), it is yours to keep. A second kind of micro-level knowledge falls into the category of local lore. This type of micro-level knowledge varies from location to location and includes such things as how to reroute a print job from a jammed network printer to one that is working, how to run a specific CD-ROM on a stand-alone workstation, or knowing the password that lets you logon to the network as an administrator. Local micro-level knowledge is picked up on the job and is usually passed between staff members by word of mouth or through e-mail. (One challenge for the manager is making sure that local micro-level knowledge is passed along to everyone who needs it. Too often such knowledge is passed around hit or miss, resulting in a public-service staff divided into knowledge haves and have nots. Chapter 10, "Communicating with Staff & Staff Training," discusses this topic in more detail.)

While some micro-level knowledge is necessary, a manager also needs a certain amount of macro-level knowledge. By this I mean a basic (not technical) understanding of how computers and computer networks function. The amount of macro-level knowledge a manager needs varies from situation to situation. Managers with a competent and cooperative in-house systems department—one that responds immediately to any call for help and gets actively involved in cooperative long- and short-term planning—can get away with knowing less than managers who are expected to solve all problems and do all planning either on their own or with a minimum of assistance from a distant systems-support office. Regardless of the situation, a manager should have enough macro-level knowledge to:

DISTINGUISH BETWEEN MAJOR AND MINOR COMPUTER PROBLEMS

As in the fable of the boy who cried wolf, any manager who rings the alarm bell over every minor computer problem will be ignored when a real crisis pops up. On the other hand, systems support staff will tend to respect and respond to managers who know enough (and have trained their staff members to know enough) to:

- try executing a command several times before concluding there is a problem;
- make sure that a problem affects more than a single computer before concluding that an entire system is down;
- always reboot a non-functioning computer to see if that fixes the problem (many computer problems are solved by rebooting);

- be able to tell, in most cases, whether or not a problem involving access to the Internet is the fault of the computer sitting on the desktop or the fault of some Web server that might be thousands of miles away;
- find out if someone on the spot (other public-service staff, for example) knows how to fix a problem before calling in the experts.

SUFFICIENTLY EXPLAIN A PROBLEM TO A COMPUTER TECHNICIAN

Specific descriptions of problems—"We are using Netscape 4.0 to access .pdf files. When we click on a link to any .pdf file, it gives the message 'Error 109' and the file will not load."—are appreciated more than vague complaints—"This computer isn't working worth beans."

HAVE A GOOD IDEA OF WHAT CAN AND WHAT CANNOT REASONABLY BE DONE WITH THE COMPUTER SYSTEMS AT ONE'S DISPOSAL AND APPLY THIS KNOWLEDGE WHEN LOBBYING FOR IMPROVEMENTS TO LIBRARY COMPUTER SYSTEMS

The manager who constantly asks for the impossible or the totally impractical—"Hey, why don't we control access to our public workstations by getting one of those gizmos that recognizes users by their voice patterns?"—will soon lose credibility. Before proposing any change or improvement, take a bit of time to find out if it is even possible, roughly how much it will cost, and how much work it will involve. You can often get all the information you need by posting a query to an appropriate listserv or by surfing a few appropriate Websites.[1]

RESPOND INTELLIGENTLY TO QUESTIONS OR SUGGESTIONS FROM PUBLIC-SERVICE STAFF AND USERS

As a manager of public-access computers, you will be turned to as a computer authority (even if you aren't). Having enough knowledge to explain, in general terms, the reason behind a policy—"How come library patrons can't download files to the C: drive?"—or to explain why something is simply not possible—"Why doesn't the library just scan all its books and put them online?"—is essential. Essential, too, is knowing when to say, "I don't know, but I'll find out and get back to you."

This chapter, like this book, is not intended to turn anyone into a computer expert. In fact, anyone who is a computer expert could easily skip the rest of this chapter. The purpose here is to touch on selected major concepts with which all managers of public-access computers should have some familiarity. At the end of this chapter is a list of sources you can turn to for more detailed information on computer technology or to keep up-to-date with new technologies. Change, after all, is the only constant in computer technology, and it will not be long, no doubt, before the information that follows is out of date.

BASIC COMPUTER CONCEPTS FOR MANAGERS

COMPUTER HARDWARE

Hardware is the physically tangible part of any computer device: wires, cables, chips, cases, monitors, keyboards, and so on are commonly referred to as *hardware*.

Dumb terminal

One of the simplest types of computer hardware is the dumb terminal—a monitor and a keyboard wired to a central computer (server). Because a dumb terminal relies entirely on the server for processing, it can be used only for simple data entry and retrieval. When online public-access catalogs (OPACs) first appeared on the library scene in the 1980s, dumb terminals were the only means of access to the catalog. Increasingly, libraries are replacing dumb terminals with personal-computer workstations that can perform multiple tasks. The fact that a dumb terminal connected to an OPAC can do only one thing (access the online catalog), also means that it cannot be used for such things as Web surfing, checking e-mail, playing games, and so on. For this reason, some libraries keep a few dumb terminals around as a dependable means of access to the catalog. See *thin client* under *Clients and Servers*, below.

Personal computer (PC)

The terms *personal computer* and *PC* are often used to describe any type of desktop or laptop computer capable of doing its own processing; under this definition, a Mac is a personal computer. However, *personal computer* (PC) can also be used to describe computers that conform to standards originally set by IBM and now regulated, for all practical purposes, by Intel processors and Microsoft Windows software. Such computers are sometimes referred to as *Wintel computers*. Under this second definition, a Mac is not a personal computer (PC). These two very different definitions of *personal computer* (PC) can lead to confusion if everyone is not clear which definition is being used. The term *microcomputer* is more accurate than *personal computer* when talking about both IBM-compatible personal computers and Macs.

Stand-alone computer

A stand-alone computer is any computer (usually a microcomputer) that is not permanently connected to a network. On a stand-alone computer, all software and data must reside on the computer's hard drive or on disks inserted into the computer's disk drives (which might be floppy drives, CD-ROM drives, DVD drives, or drives of some other type). Although stand-alone computers have largely been replaced by, or converted into, network computers, they are still in use. While stand-alone computers have such disadvantages as not being able to access the Internet (unless they are equipped with a modem and connected to a telephone line) and not being able to print to network printers, they are useful when the desire is to make available only certain applications (such as a specific CD-ROM database) while preventing the use of the computer for other applications (such as sending e-mail or surfing the Web).

CD-ROM tower

The CD-ROM tower—a computer with many CD-ROM drives in it—provides access to a number of CD-ROMs over a network, making it possible for more than one user to simultaneously access a CD-ROM and, in turn, obviating the need to check out CD-ROMs to users or to provide access to CD-ROMs at stand-alone workstations. Although many databases that at one time were made available primarily through CD-ROM are now served over the Web, the CD-ROM format is still useful for low-use or specialty databases and for books on CD-ROM. (See Chapter 5, "CD-ROM," for more on this topic.)

Minicomputer

A minicomputer is larger than a microcomputer (personal computer or Mac) but smaller than a mainframe. Minicomputers are often used as servers or to control entire networks. The DEC VAX and IBM AS/400 are two popular minicomputers.

Mainframe computer

A mainframe is a very large computer capable of handling hundreds of users at one time. Mainframes may be used to serve a large library catalog, to control a large network, or to serve a large Website.

COMPUTER SOFTWARE

Software consists of instructions that tell a computer what to do. When a number of instructions are strung together to tell a computer to carry out a specific task, this is called a *program* or *software program* or *application*.

Application

Application is a term often used by computer experts to mean any software program that performs a task for the computer user at the computer user's command. Word processors, Web browsers, paint programs, calculators, and spreadsheets are all examples of applications. The counterpart of an application is system software (see below).

Helper application

A help application (also called a *plug-in*) is a software application that increases the capabilities of another application. Some of the most common helper applications are those designed to enhance Web browser software. For example, Adobe Acrobat Reader is a plug-in that allows Web browsers such as Netscape and Internet Explorer to display Web documents stored as .pdf files. Many plug-ins can be downloaded for free over the Internet, but there may be a charge for the top-of-the-line version of a particular plug-in.

System Software

System software controls the inner workings of a computer and actually runs the applications. Most system software runs seamlessly, without the computer user having to tell it to do its job. Operating systems and printer drivers are examples of system software.

Operating system

The operating system (OS) is the main control program of a computer. Also know as a *platform*, the operating system runs everything on the computer and is loaded as soon as the computer is turned on. Even if no applications are running, the main part of the operating system (the kernel) resides in the computer's memory. An application (software program) must be able to communicate with the operating system in order to run, which is why an application made to run exclusively on a Mac operating system will not run on a computer using the Windows operating system (and vice versa). However, some applications are designed to run on more than one operating system, and some operating systems can emulate a different operating system in order to run an out-of-system application. There are many operating systems, but chances are you will come in direct contact with only a few of them. Operating systems can be divided into single-user and network operating systems.

Single-user operating systems

Single-user operating systems are designed to work on microcomputers and to process commands coming from a single user. The major single-user operating systems are DOS, MacOS, OS/2, and Windows.

DOS

DOS (Disk Operating System) was at one time the leading operating system for personal computers, though it has now been eclipsed by the Windows operating systems. DOS-based applications linger to this day, and it is possible to run most of them under the Windows operating systems. One disadvantage of DOS is that it doesn't lend itself to multitasking—the running of more than one computer application at one time. Another disadvantage is that DOS is text-based and offers virtually none of the graphic capabilities of either the Windows or the Mac operating systems.

MacOS

The first Mac operating system was introduced in 1984, though MacOS itself was not introduced until some years later. Offering a highly graphical operating system and efficient multitasking, Mac is a favorite of many computer aficionados though it claims only a small part (about 10 percent) of the personal computer market.

OS/2

OS/2 is an IBM operating system that runs OS/2, Windows, and DOS applications. It has both a graphical interface and a text-based interface that is similar to DOS, an operating system with which OS/2 shares many commands.

WINDOWS

Windows, a Microsoft product first released in 1985, is today the leading operating system for personal computers. Windows is actually more than one operating system. The older versions of Windows are commonly referred to as *Windows 3.X* (the letter *X* standing for the release number, as in Windows 3.1 or Windows 3.2). Windows 3.X has largely been replaced by Windows 95/98. From an end-user point of view, there is virtually no difference between Windows 95 and Windows 98 (or Windows NT, for that matter); Windows 3.X, however, is different enough that end users may need some help adjusting to a change from the older operating system to one of the newer versions. All the Windows systems offer a Mac-like graphical interface that features re-sizable, movable windows and allows for the running of more than one application at a time (multitasking).

NETWORK OPERATING SYSTEMS

Unlike the single-user operating systems described above, network operating systems can handle many users at the same time. There are many network operating systems. The ones you are most likely to come in contact with as a manager of public-access computers are Window NT, UNIX, Linux, and NetWare.

WINDOWS NT

The *NT* in Windows NT stands for "New Technology." Although Windows NT can be used as an operating system for high-end personal computers (known as "NT Workstations"), it has earned its greatest popularity as software for running computer networks both large and small. Windows NT's symmetric multiprocessing (SMP) can provide processing for hundreds of network users at the same time. The security features on NT allow a skilled NT administrator to lock down a network so that users can run only those applications and access only those files the administrator permits them to run or access. An NT administrator can also configure a network so that computers on the network share a variety of peripherals, including printers, CD-ROM towers, and even personal-computer hard- and disk drives. (Windows NT administration is a specialty field that requires significant training to master.) The earliest version of Windows NT, version 3.1, was introduced in 1993; Windows NT 2000 is scheduled for release in 1999.

UNIX

UNIX is a popular operating system for running workstations and servers, a fact which is reflected in the thousands of large Web servers running under UNIX. There are many versions of UNIX available, but all of them are written in C programming language. While there is no need for a manager of public-access computers to become a C programmer, learning a few basic UNIX commands can be useful if any of the systems you regularly work with run under the UNIX operating system.

LINUX

Linux is a freeware version of UNIX developed by Linus Torvalds. Linux runs on many different platforms, and hundreds of programs (some free, some proprietary) have been written to run on Linux. Like UNIX, Linux is an operating system used by a large number of Web servers.

NetWare

A product of Novell, NetWare is the most popular software for running local area networks (LANs). It is also widely used to run intranets. Some versions of NetWare can support up to 1,000 simultaneous users.

COMPUTER NETWORKS

Any group of interconnected computers is a network. Networks are composed of hardware (computers, cables, etc.) and software (network operating systems such as NetWare, Windows NT, UNIX, Linux, or other software capable of supporting simultaneous users). Networks usually include clients and servers. The most common types of networks are local area networks (LANs), wide area network (WANs), intranets, and internets.

Clients and servers

Many computer networks are configured in the client/server network model. To put it simply, in a client/server network, one computer can get information from another. The computer that provides the information (data, software, Web pages, etc.) is the *server*; the computer that asks for the information is the *client*. Clients can access drives on servers very much as if those drives were on the client computers themselves. Servers tend to be large, powerful computers, but even a modest personal computer can be used as sever.

The term *thin client* refers to a network situation in which the client performs little of the actual processing and functions somewhat like a dumb terminal; however, today's sophisticated thin clients can do much more than the old dumb terminals ever could, including allowing users to browse the Internet and to run Windows applications such as Adobe Acrobat Reader. The term *fat client* refers to just the opposite scenario—a network in which the clients perform a great deal of the processing and the server merely supplies the data to be processed. The term *peer to peer network* describes a network in which all the component computers are both clients and servers and in which processing is shared equally.

Server

A server is any computer in a network that supplies data (files, software, etc.) to other computers (clients). A server is, typically, a large, fast computer (possibly a minicomputer or mainframe computer) that has the processing power and operating software to handle requests from many client computers at the same time. Computers that have no function other than to act as a server are called "dedicated servers." A Web server is simply a server that serves Web pages via the

Internet. A large Website will have several dedicated Web servers, while a small Website could get by with as little as a PC acting as its Web server.

Proxy server

A proxy server is an application that lets an online user enter through one door (or "port," to use the proper computer terminology) but sends that same user out a different door. This function is important in creating firewalls and otherwise protecting servers from hackers. Proxy servers can also be used to assign IP addresses that allow authorized remote users to access proprietary full-text information resources and databases.

LAN

A LAN (Local Area Network) is a network of computers in physical proximity to one another. Often, the computers that make up a LAN are located in a single building. LANs require some type of network operating software (such as NetWare, Windows NT, etc.) as well as some kind of physical connection (Ethernet and Token Ring are the leading LAN architectures). Computers on a LAN may have the ability to share data with each other and to access shared hardware, such as printers. On a LAN with one or more dedicated servers, the server(s) can provide other computers with data and software.

WAN

A WAN is a network of computers distributed over an area as large as an entire state or country. The computers in a WAN are usually connected via telephone lines, fiber-optic cable, or satellites. Except for the size of the territory it covers, a WAN appears very much like a LAN to an end user.

Intranet

An intranet is a local area network to which access is limited to authorized users. In the classic example, a company puts internal documents, data, or software on an intranet that is configured so only the company's employees may access it. If that same intranet is connected to the Internet, company employees may then access the intranet from afar even though the general public remains excluded.

A library might use an intranet to serve internal documents, data, or software to its employees, much as a company would. A library might also serve proprietary databases over an intranet.

Internet, an

Any large network made up of smaller networks may be called an *internet*. The most famous and biggest of all internets is *the* (capital *I*) Internet, which is discussed below.

Ethernet

Ethernet is both a physical medium (cable) and protocol for transmitting data on a local area network. More LANs use Ethernet than any other architecture. Computers that share an Ethernet can communicate with each other at high speeds and, if the Ethernet is so configured, use the Ethernet as their connection to the Internet. The standard variety of Ethernet has a bandwidth of 10 Mbps (megabytes per second), with Fast Ethernet running at 100 Mbps and Gigabit Ethernet running at 1,000 Mbps. An Ethernet card is a piece of hardware that allows a computer to connect to an Ethernet.

Token ring

Like Ethernet, token ring is an architecture for running a local area network and can be used to establish a connection to the Internet. Under token ring architecture, computers on a network are arranged in a virtual ring. Any computer that wishes to send data needs to catch a constantly circling bit pattern called a *token* and attach its data to the token before sending it on its way. To the end user, the architecture of a local area network is invisible, and few people who access LANs know anything about how the LANs they use are configured.

Firewall

A firewall is a virtual boundary that prevents unauthorized access to defined areas on a network. For example, a library's catalog and its database of cardholders' home addresses might be stored on a single computer. A firewall could allow someone accessing this computer via the Web to browse the catalog while preventing that person from snooping in the address database.

CONNECTIVITY

In a general sense, *connectivity* refers to any communication between computers and terminals. The word *connectivity* is also thrown around when discussing how a person or institution is connected to the Internet. Fast, reliable Internet connections are considered good connectivity, while slow, unreliable connections are considered bad connectivity. The term *bandwidth* describes the capacity to transmit electronic data. Bandwidth can be measured in bits per second, bytes per second, or Hertz (cycles per second). "Low bandwidth" translates to a slow connection.

There are many ways in which individuals and institutions may connect to the Internet.

Modem

A modem is the most common way to connect a home computer to the Internet. Standard modems send data over telephone lines, operating at speeds as slow as 300 bits per second and as fast as 56,000 bits per second. It is now rare for libraries to use modems to connect public-access computers to the Internet, but the slowness of telephone modems comes into play when considering the needs of remote users who access library Web pages and other electronic resources from home.

Cable

With cable access to the Internet, data is sent over the same type of line used for cable television rather than over the metal wires used for telephone connection. This makes the speed of access much faster than with telephone modems. The drawbacks of cable access to the Internet are that it is more expensive than telephone access, that it is not available everywhere, and that it does not work flawlessly for making connections to online catalogs. Still, it is a good way to connect to Web pages, and some smaller libraries use cable as their main means of accessing the Internet.

Digital subscriber line

Digital Subscriber Lines (DSL) transmit over standard telephone lines but use a "splitter" to allow voice and data to travel over the same line. This means that a single telephone can be used for Internet access and regular telephone calls at the same time. DSL is about the same price as cable and is faster than ISDN (see below).

ISDN lines

An ISDN (Integrated Services Digital Network) line is a high-speed, high-capacity means of transmitting data. The highest speed ISDN lines are equivalent to T1 lines (see below). ISDN lines are connected to personal computers using a terminal adapter which is commonly called an ISDN modem, though it is technically not a modem.

T1 lines

Small and medium-sized organizations with heavy network traffic often use T1 lines to connect to the Internet. Sometimes referred to as *leased lines*, T1 lines can transmit large amounts of data much faster than the telephone lines used with standard modems. The higher the number following the *T*, the greater the capacity and speed of the line.

For example, a T1 line provides 24 64–Kbps voice or data channels, a T2 line provides 96, a T3 line provides 672, and so on.

OC 1

The OC in OC 1 stands for *optical carrier*, and OC followed by a number is used to designate the speed of high-speed, high-capacity, fiber-optic cables. The higher the number following the OC, the greater the capacity and speed of the cable. For example, an OC 1 line transmits at 51.84 Mbps, an OC 3 line transmits at 155.52 Mbps, an OC 12 line transmits at 622.08 Mbps, and so on.

Hub

A hub is a device that joins network communication lines together. One typical use of a hub is to physically join multiple network workstations to a server. A passive hub simply makes a physical connection, while an active hub regenerates and strengthens electronic signals. An intelligent hub does actual processing in the form of routing and switching electronic signals. The size and efficiency of a network's hub (or hubs) has a tremendous effect on the speed of transactions conducted on that network.

Repeater

A repeater is a computer that links together two (or more) networks of the same type. Repeaters strengthen or retransmit signals so that they can be sent over long distances without loss of quality.

Bridge

A bridge is a computer that links together two (or more) segments of a LAN (local area network). A bridge can connect two local area networks of different types, such as a Token Ring and an Ethernet.

Router

A router is a computer that moves data packets from one LAN (local area network) or WAN (wide area network) to another. A typical network hierarchy might have LANs and WANs connected to hubs which in turn connect to a router that deal packets of data up and down the Internet. The two major manufacturers of routers are Cisco Systems and Bay Networks.

ATM

In the world of networking, ATM stands for *Asynchronous Transfer Mode*, not *automatic teller machine*. ATM is a high-speed network technology that was designed to work with such older network technologies as Ethernet and Token Ring. ATM is considered to have great potential as a means of sending real-time voice and video over the Internet.

KEY INTERNET CONCEPTS

At this date, the Internet itself needs no introduction. The granddaddy of all networks, the Internet grew out of networks originally developed for the United States military. The terms *Internet* and *Word Wide Web* (also knows as *the Web* or *WWW*) are often used interchangeably, though purists point out that the two are not the same thing.

The World Wide Web is a hypermedia method of accessing sites on the Internet. Hypertext links on Web pages allow users to jump seamlessly from one Web page to another. Though the Web can be used to provide access to all kinds of data and software, the bulk of the Web is composed of pages created using HTML (Hypertext Markup Language).

HTML

HTML (Hypertext Markup Language) is the language used to create Web pages. HTML "tags" control the layout of Web pages and are used to create hyperlinks to other Web pages.

Web browser

A Web browser is a piece of software that allows users to access Web pages and to use hypertext links. The two leading brands of Web browsers are Netscape and Internet Explorer. There are other brands of Web browsers as well, including Lynx, a text-only browser which allows access to Web pages but does not display images or play sounds. Lynx is used by those with low-end computers and/or very slow modems.

A single brand of Web browser may come in different versions. These versions are usually distinguished by numbers, with lower numbers indicating an older version of a browser: Netscape 2.0 is an older version than Netscape 4.5. Different brands of Web browsers, and different versions of the same brand of browser, have different capabilities; for this reason, a Web page will look and perform differently depending on the Web browser being used to access it. Variations among Web browser need to be considered in designing Web pages and in determining how Web access to databases and other online resources will be provided. Just because a Web page looks and acts a certain way on one browser is no guarantee it will look and act exactly the same way on another browser.

ISP

An ISP (Internet Service Provider) is any organization that provides access to the Internet. ISPs can be for-profit companies such as America Online or MSN, or they can be non-profit institutions such as schools or universities. ISPs often provide their clients with e-mail accounts, access to the Internet, and space for personal Web pages.

IP address

Every computer connected to the Internet has to have a unique IP (Internet Protocol) address. IP addresses take numeric forms, such as 129.68.30.200, which can also be translated into domain names, such as *www.library.tmc.edu*. While Internet computers can have permanent IP addresses, it is also possible for them to have IP addresses that are assigned on a temporary basis (dynamic IP addresses).

There are a number of ways to determine a computer's IP address. One way is to access the Traceroute Web page at:

www.slac.stanford.edu/cgi-bin/nph-traceroute.pl

Accessing this page not only shows you the IP address of the computer which accessed the Traceroute page, it also shows the Internet route the computer followed to get to Traceroute.

IP addresses are an important element in providing remote access to proprietary databases, as many vendors grant access to their databases on the basis of IP address.

TCP/IP

TCP/IP (Transmission Control Protocol/Internet Protocol) is an Internet protocol (actually two protocols) that makes it possible for all different types of computers to communicate with each other over the Internet.

FTP

FTP (File Transfer Protocol) is a protocol that allows files to be transferred over TCP/IP networks such as the Internet. When people talk about "downloading" something over the Internet, they usually mean that they are FTPing it. Most Web browsers include a program for FTPing files, but there are also single-purpose FTP software programs such as WS_FTP.

Z39.50

Z39.50 is a national standard that, when fully implemented, will let a computer user search a distant computer database using the search syntax of his or her local computer system. Instead of needing to learn dozens of search protocols, under Z39.50 users would need to learn only one search protocol.

Telnet

Telnet is a protocol that allows a remote computer to log in to other computers on the Internet.

CGI

CGI (Common Gateway Interface) is a way of allowing someone accessing a server via the Web to run some other program on that same server. For example, CGI can be used to run forms that collect data from Web users, to verify passwords, or to allow someone to access a database. CGI employs programs called *CGI scripts*. These CGI scripts are often written in the PERL computer language.

Cookie

A cookie is a small file sent from a Web server to a client computer. Cookies have useful functions, such as making it possible for someone to access a database without logging in each time. There are some security and privacy concerns surrounding cookies, which is why most Web browsers give users the option of being warned before accepting a cookie.

Java

Java is a full-blown programming language based on the C++ language and developed specifically for use on the World Wide Web and intranets. Java programs, often called *applets*, can be launched (run) from HTML documents (Web pages) on any computer equipped with a "Java capable" Web browser. One typical use of Java is to process information collected from Web forms.

Javascript is a Netscape programming language that is supported by every version of Netscape numbered 2.0 or higher. Javascript is easier to learn than the Java programming language, but it is also less powerful. Javascript is often used in conjunction with Java, as when Javascript is used to create an online form and a Java applet is used to process the data collected by the form.

Java programs are often called "applets" because they are small applications. The term *applet* may be used to describe any small application.

FURTHER INFORMATION

Computer Currents High-Tech Dictionary
www.currents.net/resources/dictionary/dictionary.phtml

PC Webopedia
webopedia.internet.com/

Techweb TechEncyclopedia
www.techweb.com/encyclopedia/

Yahoo!: Computing Dictionaries
*dir.yahoo.com/Computers_and_Internet/Information_and_Documen-
tation/Computing_Dictionaries/*

NOTE

1. A corollary to the above caution is that almost any truly eye-popping thing you see done with a computer on television or in the movies is probably impractical if not just plain impossible. Take this recent example from the popular, and often technically accurate, television series *Law & Order*: Two television detectives seeking information about a student approach a circulation clerk in a college library. Turning to her computer, the clerk (in a blatant violation of privacy) brings up the student's circulation record, and there, on screen, is not only a list of what books the student has checked out, but her photograph as well. While it is technologically possible to include photographs as part of patron records, the cost and logistics of doing so in a real-world situation would be prohibitive in almost every case.

2 FACILITIES

The glorious idea of an Information Highway replete with ribbons of high-speed connections and shining, state-of-the-art desktop computers does not mean much without such inglorious items as the desks upon which those computers sit, the electrical outlets they plug into, and the physical space to house them all. Such workaday components of the Information Highway, here lumped under the rubric of *facilities*, are of great concern to managers of public-access computers because, without them, there can be no public access. Managing facilities can be tricky for a number of reasons, not the least of which are that most existing library buildings were not designed to accommodate computers and that budgeting for facilities is often overlooked in the rush to acquire more computers.

PHYSICAL SPACE

At least one of the reasons that libraries are thought of as good places for public-access computers is the perception (not always accurate) that libraries have plenty of prime space for computers. Why, after all, build a new campus computer lab or civic computertorium when library space is already available. Under such logic (or lack thereof), the job of wedging more and more computers into static library space falls to library managers. And one of the first questions a manager in such a situation may ask is, "How much space does a computer require?"

The answer depends a great deal on the kind of computer with which you are dealing and the use for which the computer is intended. In most cases, one personal computer[1] workstation will require a *minimum* of 25 square feet of space; however, allowing 35 or more square feet of space per workstation is not unreasonable. It is possible to crowd more computers into less space if computers are lined up cheek by jowl on long tables or placed on stand-up kiosks, but the result will look and feel crowded and may not comply with the Americans with Disabilities Act. Well-designed modular workstations can save on space without feeling crowded or hindering access, but no matter how well you economize on space, computers still take up a lot of it.

Additional space will be needed if personal computers are attached to any peripherals such as speakers, external drives, scanners, adaptive technology devices, or local printers. One of the often overlooked advantages of networked printers is that they eliminate the need to provide space for multiple local printers. Also, if the goal is to provide a true scholar's workstation environment, it is necessary to provide enough desktop space to accommodate not only a personal computer, but also the books, notes, and other tools of a scholar at work.

Dumb terminals (such as those commonly used to access online public-access catalogs) take up less space than personal computers. Dumb terminals do not have CPUs, their monitors and keyboards are narrower than those of most personal computers, they do not require space for mice, and there is no need to make room for chairs when dumb terminals are placed on stand-up kiosks, as they often are. When replacing dumb terminals with personal computers, it is likely that the space that previously accommodated the dumb terminals will be sufficient for only a smaller number of personal computers.

In the days when even a large library might have no more than a half dozen stand-alone personal computers available for public use, finding space for them was an *ad hoc* activity that involved nothing more than appropriating a likely table or study carrel and locating a handy wall socket. Given the large numbers of personal computers that libraries support today, the amount of space at stake is so great that space planning must involve all levels of library administration and staff and seek input from library users. With the exception of a new building or major expansion, adding more computers means taking away space from some other activity, and, in such a situation, sensitivity to the needs of all library users is crucial for a successful expansion.

ELECTRICAL POWER

One factor that will determine just where you can put computers is the availability of electrical power. Computers must be adjacent to their power supply. Under no circumstances should you run power cords across open floor space: the cords will trip passersby and present a fire hazard. Also, you should never use extension cords with computers whether you run the cords across open floor space or not.

When power outlets are found only along walls, as is often the case in older buildings, computers will need to go along the walls as well. If this is a problem, one solution is to have a qualified electrician install new power outlets. Often the cheapest way to provide new power outlets is to install interior power poles and run electrical wires down from the ceiling. Interior power poles are an eyesore, though they are less offensive if run down existing support columns. A more attractive solution is to install new power outlets in the floor, though this can be an expensive solution—especially if the floor is concrete. Floor outlets allow great flexibility in deciding where computers will be

Tip Sheet

Electrical Tips

Any modifications to electrical systems—including (but not limited to) moving or installing electrical outlets, moving or installing electrical wires, or making any changes to fuses or circuit breakers—must be made by qualified electricians and must meet the requirements of building codes. Electrical work is not a job for amateurs.

Also, if a large number of computers are being added to a building, check with an expert electrical consultant beforehand to make sure the building's electrical infrastructure can support the additional load. Plugging too many computers into a building with an inadequate electrical infrastructure is no less dangerous than plugging too many appliances into a single wall socket.

placed, but, just as with wall outlets, once floor outlets are installed the computers that use them must sit adjacent to the outlets. For this reason it is important to plan the location of floor outlets carefully and to allow for future needs (such as expansion).

Wherever power outlets are located, there should be some kind of surge protector between all electronic equipment and the power source into which it is plugged. Surge protectors range in price from $10 to well over $100, but, whatever the cost, it is important to have a surge protector that will clamp (limit) a voltage spike to less than 400V. The package label on a surge protector will give its clamping-voltage rating—the lower the clamping-voltage level, the more protection the surge protector offers. Surge protectors are often included in power strips, though do not assume that this is always the case or that a power-strip surge protector will have a sufficient clamping-voltage rating. Whether they offer surge protection or not, power strips are useful in and of themselves because they accommodate multiple plugs and make it easy to cut off power to an entire workstation for maintenance or other purposes. It may be possible to accommodate more than one workstation with a single power strip, but one power strip per workstation is desirable.

A superior alternative to surge protectors is an uninterruptible power supply (UPS). An uninterruptible power supply is a device that not only protects computers and their peripherals against power surges, it also continues to supply power in the case of an outage. While the length of time a UPS will continue to supply power is limited, an adequate UPS will provide enough time to safely shut down all computers before its power reserves run out. There are small UPS systems designed to support a single computer workstation, as well as larger ones that can support an entire network. You can learn about various UPS systems at *Yahoo!* Power Supplies (*dir.yahoo.com/Computers_ and_Internet/Information_and_Documentation/Product_Reviews/ Components/Power_Supplies*).

NETWORK DROPS

If a computer is networked, not only does it need to be close to a power outlet, it also needs to be close to a network drop: a small electronic box into which the networked computer clips, much as a telephone or modem clips into a modular telephone jack. The function of a network drop is to connect a computer or other electronic device, such as a printer, to a local area network. As with power cords, network cords must not be strung across open floor space. Network drops can be installed in walls, built into the floor, or dropped from a ceiling, much like power outlets.

Perhaps the most important thing to know about network drops is that you should plan for more of them than you think you will need. One rule of thumb is to count up the maximum number of networked computers you think you will ever have, double that number, and then plan for that many network drops.

FURNITURE

Computer furniture, which can range from pressed-into-service library index tables to custom-built computer workstations, supports and protects computer equipment while providing a place for computer users to work.

Too often, new computers come into a library with an inadequate— or even non-existent—furniture budget. In such cases, managers have to rely on existing library furniture which, if built for reading and writing, is too high for computer tasks and incapable of gracefully accommodating computer cords and cables. Even worse, confiscating existing desks and tables for computers is certain to raise complaints from library users who feel they are being displaced. For these reasons, any manager involved in the process of planning for more public-access computers should insist that furniture be budgeted into the plan from the outset and that it be budgeted for at an adequate level.

When working with a furniture budget, it is important to expend that budget wisely. Because computer furniture can easily cost more than the computers that sit on it, and because few libraries can afford to replace or recondition furniture very often, it is crucial to think of the long term when selecting furniture. Though it initially costs more, durable furniture will, over the years, prove a better bargain than the shoddy kind. Furniture used in a public-access setting will receive considerable abuse (some of it intentional) and so needs to be sturdier and more damage-resistant than furniture built for home use. Try to select furniture that seems flexible enough to adapt to various uses over the years. Computer furniture that is too specifically designed to accommodate a particular piece of equipment will not be of much use when that equipment has outlived its usefulness—and computer furniture *always* outlasts computer equipment.

Furniture aesthetics are important, too, as attractive furniture can improve the atmosphere of a computer area and offset the typically unaesthetic look of computers. Because beauty is in the eye of the beholder, it is a good idea to seek input from many sources when settling on furniture styles and colors. Forming a furniture-selection committee comprised of library staff, library users, your architect (if you are working with one), or anyone at your institution who has had experience selecting or purchasing institutional furniture is a good way to get input. Making field trips to other libraries or computer labs is also a good exercise. When you go, make it a point to ask about any problems with durability or functionality. Furniture company sales representatives are usually knowledgeable about matters of furniture function, style, and design and will provide their advice free of charge (if not free of bias towards the product lines they sell).

As a rule, it is best to choose classic styles and neutral colors that will endure the swings of furniture fashion. If the resulting look seems boring, just think of all those burnt-orange and avocado-green chairs now relegated to the darkest depths of the stacks and remember that they were once all the rage. Whatever style of furniture you settle on, steel yourself to the fact that there will be complaints about how ugly it is and about how much money was *wasted* on it. You cannot please everyone when it comes to furniture.

Computer furniture that contributes to computer security is preferable to furniture that does not. Workstations that rise up to block the computer user from ready view (in the manner of a traditional study carrel) are a security concern because they provide cover for all sorts of undesirable behavior. At the same time, such furniture makes it difficult for computer users to catch the attention of library staff when they need help. In public-access settings where theft is a significant threat to computers and their peripherals, furniture that provides places to which security cables can be well secured is desirable, as is computer furniture with lockable compartments. Remember, though, that computers need to be able to dissipate the heat they generate, so any compartment, locked or not, that does not provide adequate ventilation may cause equipment to overheat. Modular computer furniture that comes with built-in electrical outlets and accommodations for network drops can cut down on cord clutter and eliminate the need to run cords and cables under desks where seated users can tangle their feet in them. Although not actually furniture, cable ties are an accessory no computer cluster should be without. The best cable ties are the nylon variety which come in both reusable and non-reusable forms and are available from large computer-supply stores and catalogs.

Whether or not computer hardware is locked down, it should be easy to access once it has been placed in its furniture. Furniture should be so designed that users can easily reach disk drives, attached printers, scanners, or other peripherals. Library staff should be able to perform computer maintenance without having to dismantle the furniture to get at cords, cables, and CPUs.

Compliance with the American's With Disabilities Act (ADA) is also a consideration when purchasing library furniture, and vendors should be able to tell you whether or not their furniture complies with the ADA. For computer furniture, the most important ADA-related concern is wheelchair accessibility. As a general rule, for a workstation to be wheelchair accessible the bottom of the desktop should be at least 27 inches above the floor while the top of the desktop should be no more than 34 inches above the floor. Desktops that can be raised and lowered by means of a crank are a good way to ensure accessibility. Wheelchair-accessible workstations should be marked with the blue-and-white international symbol for accessibility and wheelchair users should have priority (though not exclusive) use of such workstations. While wheelchair-accessible workstations should not be segregated off by themselves, they should be put close to computer-cluster entrances so that there is no need to pass through the entire cluster to get to the workstation. To allow room for maneuvering wheelchairs, provide 36 inches between the back of the wheelchair-accessible desk and the front of any wall or desk behind it; if someone will be seated directly behind the wheelchair, allow 60 inches between desks.

Focus On:

Curb Cuts

Are you familiar with curb cuts? Curb cuts are those gently sloping breaks in the curb that you see at intersections and crosswalks. Although specifically designed to help wheelchair users move from street to sidewalk and sidewalk to street, they have proven to be a benefit to more than just wheelchair users: The elderly, small children, those temporarily on crutches, people wheeling suitcases or shopping carts, and many others have benefited from the convenience provided by curb cuts.

Accommodations that assist the disabled are like curb cuts in that they often help more than the fragment of the population they were originally intended to serve. For example, a workstation built extra-high to accommodate a wheelchair might also be of benefit to very tall people who have trouble squeezing their knees under a regular sized desk. A reading machine can be as much a benefit to those with literacy problems as it is to the blind. Voice-controlled software may be appreciated by everyone from a quadriplegic to a senior citizen with a touch of arthritis to a weekend athlete recovering from a wrist injury.

While it is good public service for libraries to provide as many curb cuts as possible, it is mandatory for libraries to comply with the Americans with Disabilities Act (ADA). Although there is a tendency among managers to moan about the expense and difficulty of complying with the ADA, it is important to keep in mind that a key point of the ADA is the notion of "reasonable accommodation." While the exact meaning of reasonable accommodation is open to interpretation, in practice it makes the ADA less burdensome than the many ADA-compliance horror stories would have you believe. For example, reasonable accommodation does not mean that every single workstation in a building has to accommodate a wheel chair, only that some (perhaps as few as one) do. Nor is it mandatory to have a reading machine at every workstation, a TDD system on every telephone, or Braille lettering on overhead signs.

The ins-and-outs of the ADA are too much to cover in detail in this book. A good source of information on providing service to the dis-

Continued

abled is Courtney Deines-Jones' *Preparing Staff to Serve Patrons with Disabilities*.[2] For information on ADA compliance and related disability issues, there are a number of useful Websites, including:

ADA-Related Documents and Websites
www.adata.org/adaweb.htm

- Americans with Disabilities Act Document Center
  janweb.icdi.wvu.edu/kinder

- ADA Reference Library
  handicap.bfn.org/public/ada.html

- CODI (Cornucopia of Disability Information)
  codi.buffalo.edu/graph_based

- Disabilities and Computing Program Publications
  dcp.ucla.edu/resources/publications.htm

- Law Libraries and the Americans with Disabilities Act: Service to Disabled Patrons
  www.law.utexas.edu/staff/rweston/ada-htm.htm

In addition to the above resources, the Association of Specialized and Cooperative Library Agencies (a division of the American Library Association) has produced two helpful print publications on the ADA and Libraries: *ADA Library Kit: Sample ADA-Related Documents to Help You Implement the Law*[3] and *The Americans with Disabilities Act: Its Impact on Libraries and the Library's Response in "Doable" Steps*.[4]

WORKSTATIONS SPECIFICS

Desktops

The desktop of a computer workstation should be at least 30-inches wide by 24-inches deep. There should be 24 inches of leg room beneath the desk, and, in the best of all possible worlds, legs should not have to share the space beneath the desk with CPUs, power strips, and cables. Computer desktops should be 24- to 26-inches high (the traditional work desk or library table is 29-inches high). Adjustable-height desks will benefit those shorter or taller than average, but adjustable desks cost more than comparable fixed-height desks and, for some such desks, adjustments may require significant effort.

VDT placement

It is generally accepted that the top of a VDT (video display terminal, aka, "the monitor") should be no higher than eye level; in addition, there is evidence that VDTs placed below eye level produce less strain on the eyes and neck. For most users, the common practice of placing the VDT on top of the CPU raises the screen above eye level and so should be avoided. Desk-and-computer combinations that allow VDTs to rest either directly on the desktop or below desktop level are a good way to get display screens down to the proper level. Tiltable VDTs can provide a more comfortable sight angle than those that sit on inflexible bases and can also be adjusted to reduce glare from overhead lights. The best viewing distance for a VDT varies from 18 to 24 inches; slide-out keyboard trays are useful for achieving a comfortable distance.

Keyboards

Keyboards should be movable and have fold-down "legs" for adjusting the keyboard to a comfortable angle. The keyboard should be at elbow height when a seated user's arms are dropped to the sides. Proper keyboard height can be achieved by using adjustable-height chairs and/or desks. Slide-out keyboard trays (especially the adjustable-height variety) help place keyboards at the proper height. Some keyboard trays can be retrofitted onto existing desks and tables. If you use keyboard trays, make sure they are wide enough to accommodate both the keyboard and the mouse (with mouse pad), as the keyboard and mouse should always be at the same height and adjacent to each other. Also, a mouse that can be easily moved to the left-hand side of the keyboard will be appreciated by the roughly 10 percent of the population that is left handed.

Chairs

One of the basic rules of good ergonomic design is that users should be able to change position frequently. Any furniture that locks a user into one position—as does the classic wooden library chair—is going to be uncomfortable when used with a computer. The best chairs for computer workstations roll, swivel, can be easily adjusted, and are padded. Swivel chairs with casters make it easy for users to establish a comfortable distance between themselves and VDTs, and to make the periodic changes in position that are crucial to good ergonomics. So that chairs can roll properly, casters should be appropriate for the floor surface beneath the chair. Adjustable-height chairs can help users position themselves so that keyboards and monitors are at the proper height, though very short users will find their feet dangling above the floor while very tall users will end up with their knees high and their legs at an awkward angle. Footrests will help shorter users, but only higher desks will help the very tall. Besides adjusting for height, the best computer chairs adjust for seat-pan tilt, have adjustable backrests, and have adjustable tilting tension. All adjustments should be easy to make (no tools required) and should be as intuitive as possible (users shouldn't have to turn over the chair to read complicated adjustment instructions printed underneath the seat). Chairs with high arms can force users to keep their arms at an unnatural angle and should be avoided; chairs without arms or with recessed arms that slope backward are the best option. As for padding, the "0–1–2–3 Rule" applies: brief tasks require chairs with 0 inches of padding; tasks that take 30 to 60 minutes require 1 inch of padding; tasks that take 1 to 2 hours require 2 inches; tasks that take more than 2 hours require 3 inches. Seat pans should be slightly concave and have a rounded "waterfall" edge that does not cut off circulation in the legs.

Lighting

Computer users typically need a level of lighting that allows them to:

- Read video display terminals (VDTs).
- Identify keyboard keys.
- Read printed texts placed on the desktop.

The difficulty this presents is in creating a level of light sufficient for identifying keys and reading text but not so high that it causes glare or discomfort when looking at VDTs. One solution is to outfit overhead lights with diffusers (such as parabolic wedge louvers) that prevent light from traveling horizontally into eyes or VDT screens. Glare screens mounted on VDTs may achieve the same end as diffusers, but glare screens are often more expensive than diffusers, can produce dimming or blurring, and are susceptible to theft and damage. Glare can also be reduced by:

- Positioning VDTs so they are parallel to overhead lights and perpendicular to windows.
- Using neutral (not bright) wall colors.
- Eliminating or covering shiny-surfaced objects.

In the end, it may be necessary to lower the level of light in computer areas. Offices and other institutional workspaces are commonly lit from 50 to 100 foot-candles, while a level of only 28 to 50 foot-candles is recommended for working with video display terminals.[5] Light levels can be reduced by covering windows (with baffles, venetian blinds, draperies, shades, or filters), by reducing the number of bulbs or fluorescent tubes in overhead light fixtures, or by turning off some fixtures entirely. Quite often, all the fluorescent lights on a building floor are controlled by a single switch; however, any fluorescent lights over a computer area should be controlled by a local switch. Because fluorescent lights cannot be dimmed, it is good practice to have at least some incandescent overhead lights installed in a computer area and to have these lights controlled by a local dimmer switch. This provides more control over lighting levels and is especially important in areas (such as electronic classrooms) where computer projection devices may be used. If reducing light levels makes a room too dark for reading, desktop task lighting may the answer.

Good ergonomics[6]

Comfortable chairs, proper workstations, and appropriate lighting all fall under the rubric of *ergonomics*. While there is no single, simple formula for creating ergonomically correct workstations (especially given all the various shapes and sizes of users who avail themselves of public-access workstations), you should always keep in mind these two basic rules of good ergonomics:

1. Users need to be able to change position frequently, so anything that forces someone into a rigid, inflexible position should be avoided.
2. Any piece equipment or furniture that is adjustable is going to be more comfortable than one that is not.

A number of ergonomic devices, including wrist rests, mouse support trays, forearm supports, alternative keyboards, alternatives to mice, monitor arms, and document stands may increase user comfort, though the jury is still out on the true effectiveness of some of these items. Research would be in order before running out and acquiring

Focus On:

Below-Desk VDTs

One furniture alternative that some libraries have adopted is the type of glass-topped desk in which the computer and video display terminal reside below desktop level.

Advantages:

- Offers lots of space for books and notes.

- Protects computers from spills and other mishaps.

- Provides a great deal of privacy for whatever is displayed on the VDT (useful for testing situations and for reducing complaints about objectionable Web viewing).

- Makes it easy for computer users to see staff (and vice versa).

- Is amenable to both non-computer and computer uses.

Concerns:

- Reports that the desks are uncomfortable after the first hour or so of use.

- Glare on the glass top (some desks come with removable glare hoods).

- Problems keeping the glass clean.

- Inaccessibility of VDT brightness and contrast controls.

- Difficulty accessing computer for maintenance.

- Lack of leg room.

- Small text may be harder to read on a relatively distant below-desk VDT. (This problem may be alleviated by setting VDTs to display at a larger size—for example, 800×600 instead of 640×480—and by selecting larger font sizes.)

any ergonomic device in bulk. Also note that portable items like wrist rests and document stands can vanish at an alarming rate in a public-access setting.

Another ergonomic consideration is HVAC—heating, ventilation, and air conditioning. Computers produce heat, so any area that contains a large number of computers needs a lot more cooling than the same space without computers. Similarly, if a large number of people gather in one place to use computers, increased ventilation is needed to keep the air fresh. Get expert help to determine how much heating, cooling, and ventilation is required in a computer area. The key for managers is to think about HVAC during the planning stages of any computer expansion and to bring in the expert help sooner rather than later. Changes to HVAC systems can be costly, so there is no point in thinking about them after the budget has already been expended.

Finally, libraries and computer labs sometimes use "anti-ergonomics" as a way to discourage those who would monopolize computer resources. Uncomfortable chairs, bad lighting, and undersized desks are certainly one way to increase workstation turnover. While such tactics may sometimes be justified—as in the case of providing a limited number of stand-up "express" workstations—anti-ergonomics is not good general policy.

Where to put the workstations?

As a manager, you may not have much control over where the computer workstations go in your library. Library administrators may designate a specific room or area as *the* one place where the computers will go. Computer location may be dictated by the availability of power outlets and network drops. Or computers may go by default in the reference area because that is where the public-service staff is located. When there is an opportunity to choose where computers will go, as during major remodeling or new construction, weigh the following factors into your decision:

Centralized versus decentralized

Library computers are often centralized in computer clusters (aka, "computer labs" or "computer centers"). Centralizing computers in clusters is advantageous because it can:

- Minimize the cost of running network cables and power lines.
- Maximize the efficiency of modular computer furniture.
- Facilitate the use of shared network devices (printers, scanners, and so on).
- Make it easier for staff to provide assistance to users.
- Make it easier for staff to keep an eye on computer equipment.

Focus On:

Stand Up, Sit Down

Placing computers on stand-up kiosks offers both advantages and disadvantages.

Advantages:

* Stand-up kiosks generally allow more computers to fit into less space than do sit-down desks.

* Stand-up kiosks let you avoid the added expense of supplying chairs.

* Stand-up kiosks promote a faster turn-around than do sit-down computers and are appropriate for express workstations as well as for single-purpose computers supporting applications that do not normally require a long time to execute, such as searching an online catalog, checking e-mail, and so on.

Disadvantages:

* Stand-up kiosks can present insurmountable barriers to children, the disabled, and the elderly.

* Computer users will inevitably drag chairs from elsewhere so they can sit down at stand-up kiosks.

* Stand-up kiosks are not practical for word processing and other computer projects that typically require a long time to complete.

For most public-access situations, some mixture of stand-up and sit-down computer workstations is the best solution.

---

* Isolate computer activity from other library activities (such as quiet study and reading) with which it is not compatible.

All the advantages of centralized computers are lost when computers are scattered around a building; in particular, isolated, unwatched computers are so vulnerable to theft, physical harm, or hacking that the occurrence of at least one of the three is all but inevitable. Nevertheless, the notion of computers spread around the stacks, reference rooms, and all the other places where library users work has appeal—if for no other reason than it reinforces the idea that computers are an integrated part of the library and the research process, not some entirely separate thing to be segregated into its own ghetto. While it may not be practical to scatter large numbers of computers around a library, placing at least a few handy workstations far from the main computer clusters is worth considering.

Layout

Should you opt for a centralized computer cluster, you need to think about how it will be laid out. Computers placed in straight rows generally allow the most workstations to fit into the least amount of space and is a good configuration for teaching (assuming all workstations face the same direction). However, as mentioned above, a straight-row layout can feel crowded and reduces privacy. Alternatives to straight rows include diagonal rows (which work nicely with some modular computer furniture), square pods, circular layouts, and horseshoe layouts. Spending time in a space visualizing how computer workstations might be laid out in it, perhaps using masking tape to mark off spaces where the workstations might go, is a worthwhile exercise. Remember that there should be 44 inches between rows—enough space for two adults to walk side by side or for a wheelchair to pass through and corner. Also, if a room will be used for teaching, leave room for a teacher's workstation at the front of the room. Space for a staff workstation or service desk may be needed for public-access computer clusters; these should be located where staff can best see, and be seen by, computer users.

Noise

Wherever computers go, there is going to be noise. Computing is an *activity*, and the more computers there are in one place, the more humming of CPUs, clicking of keys, whirring of printers, and buzzing of conversation there is. While amenities like carpeting, acoustic tile, and printer covers can help reduce computer-related noise, it is wise to not place a large numbers of computers near quiet areas if the intention is for those quiet areas to remain quiet. Locations near an entrance can be good sites for computer clusters since entrance areas are usually noisy to begin with. Another plus is that placing computers near an entrance makes them easy for users to find. One caveat here is that computers located too close to an entrance are susceptible to theft. Locating computer clusters in remote back areas is another possibility, but if foot traffic has to pass through quiet areas to get to the computer clusters, quiet space will be violated.

Walling off computer clusters into separate rooms is an effective way to combat noise. While almost any type of floor-to-ceiling wall will keep computer noise from invading other parts of a building, glass walls and glass doors are worth considering because the visibility they provide enhances the security of computer rooms. Opaque walls, on the other hand, have the advantage of blocking light coming from outside the computer room, thus making it possible to darken the room to the lower light level that is preferred for working with computers. Rolling walls—either soft accordion-type walls or rigid multi-panel folding walls—offer flexibility in walling off computer clusters. A rolling wall, for example, allows you to wall off a computer cluster (or part of a computer cluster) for a class session and then open it back up when the class is over. In general, rolling walls do not block sound as well as permanent walls.

DUAL-PURPOSE COMPUTER CLASSROOM

The advantage of a dual-purpose computer classroom is that when the room is not being used for classes, it can be used as a regular public-access computer cluster. This not only gets the most use out of the classroom computers, it also heads off complaints by users who want access to classroom computers when the classroom is not in use and other computer areas are full. Dual-purpose computer classrooms can work, but there are potential problems that must be addressed.

One typical difference between classroom computers and public-access computers is that classroom computers often allow users more privileges than do non-classroom computers. For example, classroom computers may grant users the privilege of downloading files from the Internet to the hard drive, or the privilege of accessing a utility (such as Windows Explorer or the DOS prompt) that allows users to delete, rename, or move files on the hard drive. While such privileges may create few problems in the controlled setting of a classroom, granting those same privileges to largely unsupervised public-access users is a recipe for disaster. Any computers that are not hacked to death in the first few weeks will likely be wiped out by user errors. Another typical difference between classroom computers and public-access computers is that classroom computers may have certain software programs that are licensed only for instructional use. Granting users the privilege to access such software in a non-classroom setting is a blatant violation of the license agreement.

The above problems are not insurmountable. For example, in a computer classroom operating under (for example) Windows NT, you could have one set of privileges when the computers are logged in for classroom use and another, more restrictive, set of privileges for when the computers are logged in for public-access use. Every time the classroom switches from one use to the other, all the computers must be logged out and then logged in again under the appropriate set of privileges. This involves some work in configuring the privileges in the first place and in doing the actual logging in and out day after day, but this is much preferable to hacked computers and licensing violations.

Other problems (none insurmountable) that should be considered when setting up dual-purpose classrooms:

- Classrooms may contain equipment (computer projectors, laser pointers, white-board markers, and so on) that must be locked up every time the classroom is opened to public access. There must be a place to lock up these items and library staff assigned to do the locking up.
- Classroom furniture (especially chairs) may not be comfortable for periods lasting more than an hour or so. Also, the forward-facing layout of most classrooms is not ideal for a non-classroom setting.
- Classroom computers often print to an in-classroom printer which may not be robust enough for heavy public-access printing and which may not be integrated into the library's pay-to-print system (if such a system is in place).
- "Evicting" public-access users so that a class can begin may lead to conflicts.
- Public-access users may feel they should be allowed to use "extra" classroom computers during less-than-capacity class sessions.
- Classroom areas are often not readily visible to library staff, leaving the computers in them more susceptible to intentional harm and making it more difficult for users to get staff help when they need it.
- Access to the classroom for instructors who want to rehearse or prepare for classes will be more limited.

FACILITIES CHECK QUESTIONS

PHYSICAL SPACE

Is there at least 25 square feet per workstation?
Is there room for peripherals (printers, scanners, etc.)?

ELECTRICAL POWER

Is the building's electrical infrastructure adequate? (Consult with an expert.)
Are existing power outlets adequate?
Are new power outlets required?
    Wall, floor, or ceiling outlets?
    How many and where? (Allow for future expansion.)
Are there surge protectors for every piece of electronic equipment?
Are surge protectors' clamping-voltage ratings less than 400v?
Do we need an uninterruptible power supply (UPS)?

NETWORK DROPS

Do we need more network drops?
How many and where? (Allow for future expansion).

FURNITURE

Is furniture part of the computer acquisition/expansion budget?
    Is the furniture budget adequate?
Is the furniture we are considering durable?
Is it flexible enough to serve more than one purpose?
Do we need a furniture selection committee?
Should we visit other libraries and computer labs to see their furnishings?
What can furniture sales representatives tell us?
Will this furniture go out of style quickly?
Does this furniture contribute to computer security?
    Does it block computer users from sight?
    Does it facilitate locking down computer equipment?
    Does it give heat-producing equipment (CPUs, etc.) good ventilation?
Does furniture include built-in power outlets and spaces for network boxes?

Can users easily reach disk drives, attached printers, scanners, or other peripherals?

Can library staff easily access computer equipment once it is placed in the furniture?

Does furniture comply with the Americans With Disabilities Act (ADA)?

DESKS

Desktop at least 30-inches wide by 24-inches deep?
At least 24 inches of leg room beneath the desk?
Desktop 24- to 26-inches high?
Have below-desktop VDT desks been considered?
Would some stand-up kiosks be desirable?
Are at least some desks wheelchair accessible?

VDTS

VDTs no higher than eye-level when seated?
VDTs on tiltable bases?
VDT viewing distance between 18 and 24 inches?

KEYBOARDS

Keyboards at elbow height when a seated user's arms are dropped to the sides?
Slide-out keyboard trays?
Keyboard tray height adjustable?
Keyboard and mouse at same level.

CHAIRS

Swivel chairs with casters?
    Casters appropriate for floor surface?
Chairs adjustable for height and seat-pan tilt?
Chairs have adjustable backrests?
Chairs have adjustable tilting tension?
All chair adjustments are easy to make?
Chairs have no or recessed arms?
Chairs sufficiently padded?

LIGHTING

Diffusers (parabolic wedge louvers) on overhead lights?
VDTs parallel to overhead lights and perpendicular to windows?
Neutral (not bright) wall colors?
Shiny-surfaced objects removed or covered?
Light levels reduced?
    Windows covered?

Fewer bulbs/fluorescent tubes in overhead light fixtures?
Some fixtures shut off?
Dimmer switch for incandescent lights?
Desktop task lighting necessary?

GOOD ERGONOMICS

Does furniture allow users to change position often?
Is furniture adjustable?
Ergonomic devices needed?
    Wrist rests?
    Mouse support trays?
    Forearm supports?
    Alternative keyboards?
    Alternatives to mice?
    Monitor arms?
    Document stands?
Are heating, ventilation, and air conditioning adequate?
    Contact HVAC consultant?

WHERE TO PUT WORKSTATIONS?

Centralized clusters or decentralized workstations?
If cluster, how should it be laid out?
    Room allowed for wheelchair access?
    Room allowed for teacher/staff workstation?
Will there be noise problems from computer cluster?
    Locate computer clusters far from quiet areas?
    Use carpet and acoustic tile?
    Wall off computer clusters?

ELECTRONIC CLASSROOMS

Should classroom computers also be used as public-access computers?
    Are classroom computers secure enough to be used for public-access?
    Can classroom-only software be made inaccessible to public-access users?
    Is classroom handicapped accessible?

NOTES

1. Throughout this chapter I am using the term *personal computer* to mean any microcomputer capable of doing its own processing (i.e. DOS, Windows, and Mac microcomputers).
2. Deines-Jones, Courtney. 1995. *Preparing Staff to Serve Patrons with Disabilities*. New York: Neal-Schuman Publishing.
3. Mayo, Kathleen and Ruth O'Donnell, eds. 1994. *ADA Library Kit: Sample ADA-Related Documents to Help You Implement the Law*. Chicago: Association of Specialized and Cooperative Library Agencies, American Library Association.
4. Crispen, Joanne, ed. 1993. *The Americans with Disabilities Act: Its Impact on Libraries and the Library's Response in "Doable" Steps*. Chicago: Association of Specialized and Cooperative Library Agencies.
5. OSHA. *Working Safely with Video Display Terminals. www.osha-slc.gov/Publications/OSHA3092/osha3092.html.*
6. Some Websites with good information on ergonomics are:
   Yahoo!: Ergonomics *dir.yahoo.com/Science/Engineering/Ergonomics*
   Office Ergonomics *www.ur-net.com/office-ergo*
   OSHA Ergonomics *www.osha-slc.gov/SLTC/ergonomics*

3 COMPUTER HARDWARE

As mentioned in Chapter 1, hardware is the physically tangible part of any computer device. The thousands of items that fall under the rubric of *computer hardware* range from internal pieces such as chips, cards, and hard drives to complete products such as central processing units (CPUs), printers, and scanners. Managers of public-access computers do not need to know all the details of assembling and maintaining hardware, but knowledge of the major types of hardware and familiarity with the characteristics that make one piece of hardware faster or more powerful than another of the same type is crucial for decision making and planning. Even if your role in selecting and acquiring computer hardware is a minor one, a working knowledge of computer hardware allows you to at least make your wishes known to those in your organization who make such decisions.

MICROCOMPUTERS: BIGGER AND FASTER

For any public-access computer operation, the core piece of hardware is the microcomputer. Microcomputers are commonly referred to by the generic term *personal computers* (PCs), which in this sense includes microcomputers running under any operating system, whether it be Mac, DOS, or Windows. Although composed of wiring, chips, motherboards, and drives—all enclosed in sturdy metal cases—microcomputers are perishable goods. No matter how freshly top-of-the-line a microcomputer may be when purchased, rapid changes in computer technology will soon enough render it obsolete. The experience of the last ten or so years has shown that the typical microcomputer will have a useful life of about three years and will be obsolete in about five years. This obsolescence has nothing to do with use: a microcomputer that sits unopened in its box for five years will be worth just as much (that is, *nothing*) as if it is used hard every day for five years. There are three principal reasons why microcomputers become obsolete so quickly:

- Hard drives keep growing larger.
- RAM (Random Access Memory) keeps expanding.
- CPUs keep getting faster.

HARD DRIVES
The hard drive is the part of the computer that stores data. Hard-drive space is occupied by software programs and by the files (written documents, spreadsheets, images, etc.) that users save to hard drives.

Hard drive sizes have continued to grow over the years, in part because the cost of hard-drive space has dropped so much that manufacturers can offer more of it for less money, and in part because new software programs require ever more space. Not so long ago, it was common for a typical microcomputer to have on its hard drive no more than a word-processing program and perhaps a few smaller specialty software programs. But in the late 1990s, most off-the-shelf microcomputers come with software packages that include a full-featured word processor, a spreadsheet program, presentation software, database-creation software, graphic-art software, and a whole array of lesser and greater programs; all of which eats up a lot of hard drive space. For example, Microsoft's popular Office 97 Small Business Edition software package requires about 200 MB of hard drive space, an amount several times the total capacity of a typical late-1980s to early-1990s microcomputer's hard drive. It is telling that hard-drive size,

Tip Sheet

Old Microcomputers

With microcomputers getting faster and bigger all the time, many libraries find themselves stuck with old, near-obsolete microcomputers that have virtually no monetary value. Depending on just how obsolete the microcomputers are, they may have some value as single-purpose or limited-purpose workstations. Old semi-retired microcomputers can be configured and designated for any combination of the following:

- E-mailing/chatting

- Searching the library catalog

- Recreational Web surfing

- Running personal CD-ROMs or software

- Game playing

- Word processing

Not only do such uses extend the lives of old microcomputers, they give users an alternative if certain activities have been banned from front-line workstations. A plus for the library is that if old single-purpose workstations get hacked or are otherwise ruined, the loss is minimal.

which was once measured by the megabyte (one million bytes), is now measured by the gigabyte (one billion bytes). One byte, by the way, is equivalent to one character (letter, numeral, and so on).

RAM

RAM (Random Access Memory) is a microcomputer's workspace. RAM dictates the number and size of programs that can be run simultaneously and the amount of data that can be instantly processed. Over the years, the amount of RAM on microcomputers has expanded for much the same reasons that microcomputer hard-drive space has expanded: RAM itself has gotten cheaper and software programs have grown to require much more RAM than did the software programs of just a few years ago.

SPEED

The most common measure of microcomputer speed is the clock speed of the CPU (Central Processing Unit). CPU speed is measured in megahertz (MHz), and when comparing computers with the same type of processor (486, Pentium, Pentium II, etc.), more megahertz usually means a faster computer. But while a 500 MHz computer processes data five times as fast as a 100 MHz computer, this does not necessarily mean that it will carry out every task five times as fast. The reason for this is that clock speed is only one factor of overall computer speed. Software design, hard-drive speed, and other elements enter into the speed equation along with MHz. The situation is analogous to automobiles: the car with the highest horsepower engine will not necessarily be the fastest car on the road if it is un-aerodynamic or has a poorly designed transmission.

Another important speed factor is CPU cache, a type of very fast memory that retrieves frequently used instructions and data. There are different levels of CPU cache. Level 1 resides on the CPU itself and runs at the clock speed of the CPU. Level 2 and Level 3 caches, which may or may not be on the CPU, are additional high-speed storage and retrieval areas.

HOW MUCH HAVE MICROCOMPUTERS CHANGED?

The chart below shows how the specifications for typical off-the-shelf microcomputers have changed over the years.

Year	Processor	Speed	RAM	Hard Drive
1988	286	10 MHz	512 KB	20 MB
1991	386	20 MHz	2 MB	40 MB
1993	486	40 MHz	6 MB	200 MB
1996	Pentium	100 MHz	16 MB	.5 GB
1999	Pentium III	400 MHz	128 MB	10 GB

MHz=MegaHertz KB=Kilobytes
MB=Megagbytes GB=Gigabytes

THE RAPID PACE OF OBSOLESCENCE: WILL IT CONTINUE?

Over the next ten years, will microcomputers continue to become obsolete as quickly as they have over the last ten? Or have microcomputers at last reached some balance point where the constant upgrading to bigger and faster machines will not be the given it has been in the past? Both questions are impossible to answer without a crystal ball. While it seems logical to think, "OK, we've got a computer lab full of 400 MHz Pentium II computers with 6-gig hard drives. They are being used to search databases, surf the Web, and write research papers. *That* should last us a good, long time," the driving force behind bigger and faster microcomputers has been the growth in size and complexity of software programs. For example, Microsoft is recommending the following *minimum* hardware for running its Windows 2000 (née Windows NT 5.0), which is scheduled for release in late 1999: 300 MHz (or more) Pentium or Pentium equivalent, 128–K Level 2 cache or equivalent, and 64 MB of RAM. If software developers continue to increase the basic system requirements of the programs they write and market, those shiny 6–gig Pentium IIs could well be candidates for a trip to the Salvation Army in a few short years.

Barring a sudden and dramatic slowdown in the bigger-and-faster trend, a manager faced with purchasing microcomputers should try to acquire the fastest, most powerful microcomputers on the market and should plan on replacing those cutting-edge machines in about three to four years.

What if acquiring the biggest-and-fastest microcomputers is a budget buster? The best option in such a situation is to add up the system requirements for all the software you plan on running and then acquiring microcomputers adequate to meet these system requirements (with some room left for growth). If your minimum system requirements happen to match the capabilities of a line of microcomputers that are being phased out to make way for a new line of bigger and faster machines, you may be able to strike a good bargain with a vendor. (Note: Microcomputer manufacturers often discount lines they are phasing out just after the December holiday season.) Of course the downside of acquiring anything less than the biggest and fastest microcomputers on the market is that lesser machines will become obsolete more quickly. Replacing lesser microcomputers more frequently may, in the long run, cost more than starting out with top-of-the-line machines that have longer useful lives.

HARDWARE BRANDS

When it comes to computer hardware (microcomputers, monitors, printers, scanners, CD-ROM players, and so on) there are no absolute best brands. Some things to consider when it comes to choosing a brand of hardware include:

Written reviews

Searching the print and online literature for hardware (and software) reviews is a good practice. Publications such as *PC Magazine, Home Office Computing, PC Week, PC Computing, Byte,* and *Macworld* regularly review hardware and software. Computer reviews in library-oriented publications may be especially useful because the reviewers are more likely to share your needs and interests. Few librarian reviewers will rate a particular microcomputer high just because its built-in speakers are powerful enough to blast paint off the walls. *Computers in Libraries* (parts of which are available online at *www.infotoday.com/ cilmag/ciltop.htm*) publishes reviews as well as an annual computer buying guide. You can find other online reviews by visiting *Yahoo!*'s list of online computer magazines at *dir.yahoo.com/Computers_ and_Internet/News_and_Media/Magazines*. Whether a review is in print or online, put on your critical thinking cap when reading reviews:

- Are the reviewer's expectations of computer performance in line with the needs of your library?
- Could some hidden conflict of interest be influencing this review?
- How does this review compare to other reviews of the same or similar products?

Word of mouth

Talk to other librarians and computer-lab managers to find out what hardware brands they are using, how well they perform, and how well they hold up. Talk to the people in your own systems department. Talk to colleagues, friends, and patrons. Ask questions on an appro-

Tip Sheet

Brand Loyalty

Libraries sometimes acquire computers willy-nilly. A few Compaq 486s here. A couple of Gateway Pentiums there. However, settling on a single brand of microcomputer (or other type of computer hardware) and purchasing a large number of them at once has several advantages: it lowers the cost per machine, facilitates negotiating a service contract with the manufacture/vendor, makes maintenance and configuration much easier for in-house staff, and can reduce the confusion that may occur when users have many different microcomputers from which to choose.

priate listserv. In the end, word of mouth may be the best source of information when it comes to choosing brands.

Service and support

Find out what kind of service and support is available for a particular hardware brand and how much, if anything, this service and support will cost. Hardware that comes with good service and support, though initially more costly, may prove a better bargain in the long-term than less-expensive hardware that comes without good services and support.

Price

If everything else (including system specifications, service and support, product reputation, and reliability) is equal, then price can be your guide to choosing hardware. One caution about price: While the cost of computer hardware tends to go down over time, waiting for the microcomputers of your dreams to drop to some magical low price may prove a fool's game. By the time the microcomputers you want reach the price you have in mind, they may be so close to obsolescence as to be no bargain at all.

Focus On:

To Mac or Not to Mac

When videocassette machines burst onto the home market in the early 1980s, consumers had a choice between Beta and VHS formats. Beta clearly was the superior format, but it lost the war for consumers' hearts and minds to the extent that, today, Beta is as dead as the eight-track audio tape. To a lesser extent, the same thing happened with microcomputers. Macintosh—by most measures the superior microcomputer—has been crushed by the giant know as Wintel (Windows operating system plus Intel processor). Unlike Beta, however, Macintosh (Mac) is down but not out. Presently claiming about 10 percent of the microcomputer market, Mac enjoys great popularity among hard-core computer aficionados (who often exhibit a fierce loyalty towards the brand) and is also quite popular in the K-12 setting. In 1999, Mac staged something of a comeback when it introduced its popular iMac microcomputer; however, the extent to which Mac will cut into Wintel's share of the market remains to be seen.

Despite the generally acknowledged superiority of Mac microcomputers, it is important for public-access computer managers to consider that more people own (and are comfortable with using) Wintel microcomputers than Macs, and that some popular software programs and CD-ROMs may not be available in Mac-compatible formats.

Providing separate Mac and Wintel computer labs, or providing a mixture of Mac and Wintel computers in the same computer cluster, provides users with a choice but presents significant obstacles to the manager:

- Public-service staff must be trained in both operating systems.

- Systems staff must be able to support both Wintel and Mac microcomputers.

- Software must be purchased in both Wintel and Mac versions (if a Mac version exists).

- Some users may become confused by the availability of two types of microcomputers.

HOW MANY COMPUTERS IS ENOUGH?

In practice, the ideal number of public-access computers is similar to the ideal number of photocopy machines: not so few that there are long lines waiting to use the machines, but not so many that machines spend a lot of time sitting idle. As with photocopiers, there is no magic formula for calculating the right number of public-access computers. For example, when Wayne State University opened its new Undergraduate Library in the Fall of 1997, the building included 700 public-access computers (plus 700 additional computer-access points). With an undergraduate student population of 17,779, that works out to one public-access computer per 25.40 undergraduates. Would such a ratio of computers to users be right for your library? The answer to this question would depend on a number of factors:

- What percentage of your library's users actually use computers?
- Does the proximity of other public-access computer facilities (labs, libraries, etc.) lessen the demand for computer access in your library?
- Does your library provide access to computer and electronic-information resources that are much in demand by users?
- Do a large number of your users own their own computers? Can and do they use their own computers to access library information resources from homes or offices?

Only in-the-library experience and observation can tell you whether or not your library provides sufficient public-access computers. Some signs that there are not enough public-access computers include:

- Frequent complaints by patrons that there are not enough computers.
- Frequent requests by patrons that certain "frivolous" computing activities be banned.[1]
- Frequent questions about whether or not there are more computers somewhere else in the building.
- Long waits to use computers and/or the need to institute an around-the-clock sign-up system for computers.
- Long periods during which all the computers are in use.
- Users walking into your computer area only to turn around and walk out when they see how busy it is.
- Regular user-versus-occasional user (or user-versus-staff) conflicts over access to computers.

While there are techniques for making fewer computers go farther, such as designating some computers as express workstations, the best answer to a shortage of computers is more computers. But, just as highway departments can never build enough roads to totally prevent traffic congestion, it is unlikely that any institution could ever provide enough public-access computers to accommodate everyone all the time.

OTHER HARDWARE

Besides microcomputers themselves, there are many types of hardware you may include as part of a microcomputer workstation. Some of this hardware, such as computer monitors, is essential. Other hardware is optional. You may choose, for example, to provide Zip drives on every workstation, or you may choose to put them only on selected workstations, or you may choose not to offer them at all. For managers, the main concerns about computer hardware are reliability, durability, and cost.

KEYBOARDS AND MICE

When you acquire microcomputers, keyboards and mice generally come as part of the package. Even so, you may have options as to what type of mice and keyboards you acquire. Keyboards are relatively standard, but some ergonomic keyboards on the market are claimed to reduce repetitive-stress injuries such as Carpal Tunnel Syndrome. Before spending extra money on ergonomic keyboards, do some research to see what evidence supports claims made by the manufacturer. An adjustable keyboard tray may do a lot more for user comfort than the most expensive ergonomic keyboard. As for mice, some offer scrolling and other advanced features, but the main mouse concern for public-access managers is how to keep mice (and mice balls) from being stolen. (See Chapter 8, "Security.")

MONITORS

As with the keyboard and mouse, a monitor (aka *video display terminal* or *VDT*) usually comes as part of the microcomputer package. Chances are if you acquire Brand Y microcomputers you will also acquire Brand Y monitors, but you may have a choice as to what model of Brand Y monitor you get. The larger the monitor, the better the image quality and higher the cost, so the trick is to get a monitor that is adequate for the applications that will run on your public-access computers without purchasing too much monitor. Giant-sized, state-of-the-art monitors may be necessary for a graphic artist's workstation, but they are overkill for workstations that are used to surf the Net and write term papers.

Color monitors, which are now all but universal, originally complied with the VGA (Video Graphics Array) standard that called for a minimum screen resolution of 640×480 pixels and a 16-color display. Today, the standard is SVGA (Super VGA), which requires at least a 256-color display and screen resolutions ranging from 800×600 pixels to as high as 1024×768 pixels.

When acquiring monitors, it helps to know something about resolution and size. Resolution is measured in pixels and is expressed in figures that indicate the number of columns and rows of pixels that appear on screen. A 640×480 resolution indicates 640 columns and 480 rows. The more columns and rows of pixels, the more that can be seen on screen. While the old standard 640×480 resolution on a 13–inch screen was fine for text-based DOS applications, the recommendation for Windows applications is a resolution of 800×600 on a 17–inch screen, and a resolution of 1024×768 on a 20–inch screen is considered even better. Other than cost, the only caveat regarding large, high-resolution monitors is that, in a classroom setting, they can make it difficult for students to see teachers and vice versa.

Other considerations for monitors include the number of colors (aka *color depth*), which can range from 16 to 256 to 65 thousand to 16 million. Sometimes the number of colors a monitor supports is indicated by a third number following the number of rows and columns. An $800 \times 600 \times 256$ monitor, for example, has 800 columns and 600 rows of pixels and supports 256 colors. Larger numbers of colors require the extra memory provided by a display adapter (aka *video card*). Refresh rate (the rate at which colors are "repainted" onto the screen) will affect the quality of monitor images—the higher the refresh rate, the better the image.

FLOPPY DISK DRIVES

With the notable exception of Macintosh's iMac microcomputer, a 3.5" floppy disk drive comes as a standard feature on all microcomputers. The most common type of 3.5" floppy disk holds up to 1.44 MB of data. The once-standard 5.25" floppy disk drive is rarely seen today.

HIGH-CAPACITY DISK DRIVES

The leading high-capacity disk drives are the Zip and Jaz drives. A Zip disk can hold either 100 MB or 250 MB of data, depending on the type of Zip disk and Zip drive. The Jaz disk can hold either 1 GB or 2 GB of data, again depending on the type of Jaz disk and Jaz drive. Both Zip and Jaz disks can be read and written to just like floppy disks, and, though many times more expensive than floppy disks, they are useful for storing software programs as well as for storing large user-generated files such as image files, electronic presentations, and database files.

CD-ROM DRIVES

Once an added feature, CD-ROM (Compact Disc-Read Only Memory) drives are now nearly as much a standard part of microcomputers as 3.5" floppy disk drives. See Chapter 5, "CD-ROM," for more information on the different types of CD-ROM drives.

DVD DRIVES

A DVD disk is similar in appearance to a CD-ROM disc but holds much more data—up to 17 GB, depending on the type of DVD disk. DVD disks are the same physical size as CD-ROM discs, and DVD players can read some CD-ROM discs. Though not yet as common as CD-ROM, many predict the DVD disk will displace the CD-ROM disc over time.

LASER DISC PLAYERS

Laser discs are a somewhat outdated technology for storing full-motion video and sound. For sound and/or still image applications, laser discs have been replaced by CD-ROMs. For full-motion-with-sound applications (such as feature-length movies), laser discs have been all but replaced by DVD disks. In library settings, laser discs are notable for their part in the early stages of the Library of Congress' *American Memory* project.

SOUND HARDWARE

With ever more Websites offering sound as part of their content, the need for some way to hear those sounds grows increasingly important. Not only is music offered via the Web, but so too are lectures,

Storage Capacity of Common Disks		
Media	**Capacity**	**Page Equivalent**
5.25" Floppy	1.2 KB	462
3.5" Floppy	1.4 MB	539
Zip Disk	250 MB	96,250
CD-ROM	650 MB	250,000
Jaz Disk	2 GB	770,000
DVD	17 GB	6,545,000

historically important speeches, and a host of other sounds of significant research value. To play sounds, a microcomputer workstation needs a sound card and speakers or headphones. Sound cards are standard on just about all microcomputers sold today and older microcomputers may be retrofitted with sound cards. Small desktop speakers are usually available for less than $20.00, but they are susceptible to theft and the sounds they produce are guaranteed to draw complaints from those working nearby. Headphones are even less expensive than speakers, selling for under $5.00 in some cases, and have the advantage of more or less containing sounds to the eardrums of the listener. Headphones are even more susceptible to theft than speakers, so some sort of check-out system would be in order. Because quite a few people (especially young people) carry portable tape or CD-players that include headphones, you may find some users plugging themselves into computer sounds entirely on their own.

PRINTERS

Despite all the predictions about a paperless society, printers are still an essential part of public-access microcomputers. See Chapter 6, "Printing," for more about printer hardware and other printing-related matters.

SCANNERS

Scanners allow users to transform paper images and/or printed text into digital form. A color flatbed scanner with a maximum scanning area of at least 8.5" by 11" inches and a resolution of approximately 600 × 1200 dpi (dots per inch) will be adequate for most applications. As scanner resolution and speed (which is measured by how long it takes to scan an image or a page of text) increase, so does the cost of the scanner

Typically, a public-access scanner is connected to a single workstation that has on its hard drive not only scanning software, but also a graphics program for manipulating scanned images and a word-processing program for editing scanned text. Including a Zip drive as part of the hardware on a scanner workstation is a good idea, as scanned images quickly fill up standard 3.5" floppy disks.

Users will flock to any public-access scanner, so be prepared to set up some kind of reservation system right from the start. Despite the popularity of scanners among library users, there are some drawbacks to providing them for public access. One drawback is that users need more help with scanners than with other types of computer hardware, and once users have successfully scanned images or text, they often need help manipulating/editing what they have scanned. Another drawback is that scanners, like photocopiers, facilitate copyright violations.

If your library posts copyright warnings on its photocopiers, then you should post the same warnings on all public-access scanners. Finally, there is always the possibility that someone could use a scanner to digitize pornographic images, to manufacture fake identification cards, or conduct other illegal/undesirable activities.

VIDEO CAMERAS AND MICROPHONES

Though sending and receiving live video and sound over the Internet is still in its infancy, the cameras and microphones that allow this type of two-way communication can be quite inexpensive. Generally, a camera of this type mounts on top of the monitor and the microphone plugs into a jack on the microcomputer. Providing cameras and microphones is not common in public-access settings, but it can be done. Three problems to consider before offering this service are: theft of equipment, noise, and the large amount of bandwidth consumed by this technology.

NETWORK DROPS FOR LAPTOPS

Wouldn't it be great if anyone who owned a laptop could walk into a library, plug their laptop into a handy network port, and then use library and Internet resources just as if they were on one of the library's workstations? It would be convenient for laptop users, it would free-up existing public-access microcomputers for users without laptops, and it would save the library a bundle on hardware, software, and microcomputer maintenance. It would be great, but it is not, at present, terribly practical. Computer technology is a long way from the day when anyone with a laptop can simply plug into a strange network and zoom off into cyberspace. If a library were to provide network drops for laptops, every laptop user would need to have a network card (few would) and those cards would have to be compatible with the library's network. Even with network cards, there are a world of lesser problems to overcome, including ensuring network security, sending jobs to network printers, and instructing users on how to configure their laptops. (A laptop rule to live by: Library staff should never touch a user's laptop. If anything goes wrong, the user may try to hold the library responsible for the problem.)

The most likely candidates for a successful implementation of network drops for laptops are libraries with small, technologically sophisticated clienteles, such as you might find at a service academy or an elite engineering college. Libraries serving a large, technologically unsophisticated population would do well to forget about network drops for laptops—at least until there is some major leap forward in networking technology. All that said, there are libraries that offer some variation of network drops for laptops. A discussion of this topic on

Focus On:

It's All in the Cards

Cards (also known as "adapters" or "boards") are printed-circuit boards that extend the capabilities of microcomputers. Cards are most often internal devices that plug into the motherboard of a CPU; however, some microcomputers (especially laptops) have special ports into which you can plug a credit-card-sized card much as you insert a floppy disk into a disk drive. Such "plug-and-play" cards are sometimes known as PC cards or PCMCIA (Personal Computer Memory Card International Association) cards. If a microcomputer lacks a card of one type or another, it is usually possible to add one, though if the microcomputer is an older model it may be more cost effective to acquire a new microcomputer rather than to retrofit. Major types of cards include:

NETWORK CARDS
Network cards allow microcomputer workstations to communicate with network servers. The two most common types of networks (Ethernet and token-ring network) each require its own type of network card.

SOUND CARDS
Sound cards can play sounds through speakers or headphones and can also record sounds through internal or external microphones. The leading, though not the only, brand of sound card is Creative Lab's Sound Blaster.

VIDEO CARDS
Going by a variety of names, including *display adapters* and *graphics cards*, video cards enhance the quality of the images that appear on a monitor screen by determining maximum resolution, maximum refresh rate, and the number of colors that can be sent to the monitor. For the highest image quality, video cards must be paired with compatible monitors.

ACCELERATOR CARDS
Accelerator cards make a microcomputer work faster by taking over some of the processing normally carried out by the CPU. For example, a videographic accelerator increases the speed at which images appear on screen, thus allowing microcomputers to quickly display 3D and other complex images. Math accelerators (also known as *floating point accelerators*) speed up complex mathematical calculations.

MODEM CARDS
A modem card is simply a standard modem in the form of a card. Some laptops use plug-in modem cards.

the Web4Lib listserv group in early 1999 included a few postings by libraries claiming some success. Anyone can access and search the Web4Lib archives at *sunsite.berkeley.edu/Web4Lib/archive.html.*

What about checking out properly configured laptops to users who could then plug them into any network drop in the library? The answer to this question is another question: Does your library check out $3,000 books? If so, then your library can probably afford to take the loss when someone disappears with or destroys a laptop. Even if no laptops are lost to theft or damage, checking out laptops will result in a lot of staff time spent reconfiguring laptops that have been intentionally hacked or accidentally messed up by users. The fact is, if you are going to spend thousands on a microcomputer, it is best to spend it on a desktop model over which you can maintain at least a modicum of control; spending those same thousands on laptops will only buy trouble.

ADAPTIVE TECHNOLOGY HARDWARE

Adaptive technology (aka, *assistive technology*) is anything that maintains, increases, or improves the capabilities of a person with a disability. Whether it is due to the Americans With Disabilities Act or because your institution wants to provide good service to as many people as possible, you may find yourself in the position of acquiring and supporting adaptive technology hardware. Some of the more common devices are:

- Magnifying screens which display text and images at large sizes.
- Closed circuit television for enlarging text and images.
- Alternative keyboards, mice, joysticks, and other means of inputting commands and information.
- Touch-screen monitors.
- Voice-recognition and voice-output technology.
- Reading machines.
- Refreshable Braille displays and Braille printers.

As with other innovations intended to help people with disabilities, adaptive technology devices may prove helpful to more than their intended population.[2]

To learn more about adaptive technology, visit Trace Research & Development Center (*www.trace.wisc.edu*) or Adaptive Technology Resource Centre (University of Toronto) (*www.utoronto.ca/atrc*).

ACQUIRING HARDWARE

While the job of actually acquiring hardware more often falls to systems staff than to public-service staff, it is worth knowing a few things about the process. The first things to learn are the particulars of your local situation. In your organization, are computer-purchasing decisions made by staff in your library, or are they made at a higher level, perhaps by an organization-wide systems or purchasing department? Are hardware decisions made exclusively by systems staff, or do public-access staff have some say in the matter? Does your organization have the freedom to shop around for computer hardware, or are you obligated to use particular contract vendors? Is there a bidding process that must be followed? How long does it normally take from the time the decision to purchase new computers has been made until they are actually up and running? The answers to these and other local questions are usually found only by asking. Heads of systems departments, purchasing officers, and old timers who have been through the acquisition process before are likely sources of information.

Some general points to consider when acquiring hardware:

YOU ARE THE CUSTOMER

Too often, those charged with purchasing computer equipment for libraries and other public institutions forget that they are customers and that vendors have an obligation to treat them well. The fact that the money to pay for the purchase may be tax dollars or grant money does not make a library or school any less important than a vendor's private-sector customers. Be reasonable when dealing with vendors, but remember to insist on fair treatment, good service, and quality products.

DISCOUNTS

Most vendors will offer educational/non-profit discounts, as well as volume discounts. Hardware manufacturers and large vendors often have special sales departments just for educational/non-profit customers; if not, make sure the salesperson you are dealing with is aware of any educational/non-profit status your institution may have.

WARRANTY

As with any major purchase, check out the warranty. How long does it last? Does it cover parts? Labor? Shipping? Will the vendor provide replacement equipment while hardware is in the shop? What is considered normal wear and tear? Can excessive use (as defined by the manufacturer) void the warranty?

SERVICE CONTRACT

Unless your in-house systems office is willing and able to make all hardware repairs, a service contract is a must. Service contracts may be included in the purchase price or may be available for an extra fee. Questions to ask about service contracts are similar to those asked of warranties. In addition, be sure the service contract includes a firm turn-around time for repairs.

INSURANCE

Many libraries or their parent institutions (schools, universities, library systems) have insurance policies that cover theft or catastrophic loss of equipment. If your library or parent institutions does not have such coverage, or if coverage excludes computer hardware, you should at least investigate the possibility of insuring computer hardware.

DELIVERY DATE

When you contract to buy or lease computer hardware, be sure that the contract includes a firm date by which the hardware must be delivered. Without a firm delivery date, it is too easy for vendors to give priority to other orders.

BUYING VERSUS LEASING

While it is more common for libraries to buy computer hardware rather than to lease, leasing is an option worth investigating. It is possible that leasing may be cheaper and include a more favorable service agreement than an outright purchase. The disadvantage of leasing is that the library will end up with no hardware when the lease runs out. On the other hand, being left in possession of a collection of obsolete hardware (and being told make do with it by budget-conscious administrators) is in some ways worse than being left with no computer hardware at all.

RECONDITIONED MICROCOMPUTERS

Acquiring reconditioned microcomputers is one way to stretch hardware budgets. While there is no simple formula for determining if a reconditioned microcomputer is a bargain, it is important to consider: 1) the price and power of a reconditioned versus new microcomputer; 2) the warranty that comes with reconditioned machines; and 3) your system staff's capacity to make repairs if/when there are problems. Remember, too, that even perfectly reconditioned microcomputers are further down the road to obsolescence than new microcomputers, and so will have a shortened useful life.

Another money-saving alternative is in-house reconditioning of your existing microcomputers. This may involve adding more RAM, up-

Tip Sheet

It's a Clean Machine

If the systems department does not take responsibility for keeping computer hardware clean, the job most likely will fall to the public-service staff. Set up a regular schedule for cleaning monitors, keyboards, and any other hardware that collects dust, dirt, or fingerprints. Keep cleaning supplies on hand and make sure that whatever products you use are approved for use on electronic equipment. Supplies should include lint-free towels, spray solution for cleaning monitor screens, hand vacuums with crevice attachments, and canned air for blowing dirt out of keyboards and other hard-to-reach areas.

grading processors, and/or installing new hard drives. Again, there is no simple formula for determining if reconditioning is worth the cost of the new parts and the labor. Just remember that if the cost of reconditioning adds up to anything close to the cost of new microcomputers, it is better to go with new machines.

TYPES OF VENDORS

The three main types of computer-hardware vendors are manufacturers, computer stores, and mail-order suppliers. Each have their strengths and weaknesses. Manufacturers can offer low prices and provide extensive support. Good computer stores can come up with creative microcomputer packages and can provide a local presence that is sometimes lacking when dealing with national/international manufacturers. Mail-order suppliers of the type found in computer-shopper catalogs do not provide much if anything in the way of service and support, but they can offer good bargains for buyers who know exactly what they want. Any of the above may also sell computers over the World Wide Web. It is certainly worthwhile to shop the Web for computer bargains, just be sure that you are dealing with a legitimate vendor.

NOTES

1. With the notable exception of complaints about pornography, when library users ask that certain computer activities (chat, e-mail, game playing, etc.) be banned, it is not the activity itself that bothers users, but rather the fact that they themselves cannot access a computer. When there are enough computers to go around, no one ever complains about chat, e-mail, game playing, and other harmless, though possibly trivial, computing activities. It is important to remember that the root cause of complaints about such activities is a lack of computers, not the activities themselves.

2. The June 1999 issue of *Computers in Libraries* is devoted to the topic of adaptive technologies and is an excellent source of information for anyone interested in the topic. Many of the articles from the June 1999 issue are available on the Web at *www.info today.com/cilmag/jun/cilmag.htm.*

4 SOFTWARE

To provide truly useful public-access computers, choosing the right software is as important as choosing the right hardware. Even the best, most up-to-date hardware is almost worthless if it is loaded up with software that is outdated, badly designed, or does not meet users' needs.

As important as software choices are, sometimes such choices are foregone conclusions. Microcomputer operating system software, for example, is preordained by the type of hardware (Wintel or Mac) on hand. In other cases, though, there are many software choices. If, for example, you choose to offer word-processing software on public-access computers, you will need to choose among such brands as Word Perfect, Microsoft Word, and so on. When you decide on a particular brand of software, you must then choose which version (also known as *release*) you want to offer. Different versions of the same software are usually numbered, with a higher number indicating a newer release (version) of the software. Word 2.0, therefore, is older than Word 6.0, which itself is older than Word 97 (which breaks the traditional numbering system by using the year of release to identify the version). Note that the newest version of a software is not *necessarily* the best version, as software companies (much like automobile manufacturers) have been known to "improve" a perfectly good product to the point of uselessness. On the other hand, beware of any software that is labeled as a "Beta release." A Beta release is a test version of a software program and likely comes with a full ration of bugs.

More fundamental than which brand or version of software you choose to provide is the question of whether or not you want to provide a particular type of software at all. Do you even want to provide word-processing software on public-access computers? Perhaps word-processing software is a feature that many users have said they want. Maybe the addition of word-processing software will further your library's goal of transforming its public-access computers into true multipurpose, scholar's workstations. But when a single user sits down for a three or four hour stint of word processing, it is going to reduce the availability of workstations for other users. And what about supporting all the printing that could potentially come out of those word processors? How will you train staff to help users of word processors? How much help are you going to provide for users of word processors? Will you install word-processing software on all of the public-access workstations, or only some?

Asking all of these questions is not to suggest that word processing should or should not be offered in public-access computer labs. The point is that the decision to provide a particular software application to the public is one that you should make mindfully. In many ways, the serious questions underlying software acquisition are the same questions underlying the acquisition of books, journals, and other library materials:

- How do we expend limited resources to provide the most good for the largest number of people?
- Which of our resources are core resources and which are expendable?
- What resources are most appropriate for our user population?
- How do we determine what resources our users most want and need?
- What mechanisms can we put in place to determine which resources are used most often?
- How do we handle user requests for new resources?
- Under what circumstances do we say "no" to a resource which many users want but which, for whatever reason, we feel we cannot or should not provide?
- How do we anticipate what resources will be needed in both the near and distant future?
- When is the right time to weed the old and replace it with the new?
- What level of user training and/or assistance will we provide for a particular resource?

Given the similarities between the acquisition and management of software and the acquisition and management of traditional library materials, managers of public-access computers would do well to adopt some of the established practices of collection-management librarians. For example, much like a traditional collection-management advisory committee, a software advisory committee composed of library staff and users can be useful for guiding software acquisitions. A written software-acquisition policy modeled on traditional library collection-management policies is a good idea as well. Such a policy spells out the objectives of a software-acquisition program and establishes criteria for evaluating, deploying, selecting, and de-selecting software. A written software-acquisition policy is also a valuable resource when dealing with user complaints regarding what software is or is not offered on public-access workstations.

One important difference between traditional library materials and software is that virtually all traditional library materials are acquired for public use. All software, however, is not intended for direct use by the public. Those types of software which the public uses directly fall under the heading of *application software*; conversely, *system software* includes software which is not used directly by the public but which runs behind the scenes to support the use of public-access computers.

SYSTEM SOFTWARE

OPERATING SYSTEM SOFTWARE

The single most important piece of system software for microcomputer workstations is the operating system. As mentioned above, operating-system software is determined by hardware, and, for the most part, the choice lies between either Mac or Windows operating systems. Operating-system software is discussed in more detail in Chapter 1, "What Does a Manager Need to Know About Technology?").

SECURITY SOFTWARE

Security software allows administrators to lock down workstations in order to prevent users from accessing critical system files, uploading viruses, or otherwise committing computer no-nos. While security protection is, in theory, optional, any public-access workstations operating without some kind of protection would soon be out of commission.

Besides protecting workstations, security software often offers other features which managers may find useful. The WinU security software, for one of several possible examples, allows system administrators to set time limits on any application and to logoff users from a remote location (such as a service desk). Security software is discussed in more detail in Chapter 8, "Security."

MENUING SOFTWARE

Similar to security software, menuing software presents users with a list of applications that are available to them and prevents (or at least hinders) access to forbidden applications. A well-designed menu makes it easy for users of public-access computers to get started without having to ask what applications are available and how they can be accessed. Everybody's Menu Builder (*www.carl.org*) is a classic example of menuing software, but many security-software packages offer menuing capability.

METERING SOFTWARE

Metering is a somewhat slippery term with two different meanings. One type of metering involves counting and controlling the number of persons simultaneously using an electronic resource (application, database, full-text document, etc.). The purpose of this type of metering is to comply with the license agreements of those electronic resources that specify a limited numbers of simultaneous users.

The other meaning for metering involves keeping a record of how frequently various electronic resources are accessed. The purpose of this second type of metering is to gather statistics that can be used for electronic collection development and for estimating hardware and staffing needs.

As a rule, software that does the first type of metering also does the second type. A number of commercially available software packages can carry out metering functions. SofTrack (*www.elronsoftware.com*), AppMeter II (*www.funk.com*), WRQ Express (*www.wrq.com*), and License Broker (*www.sintegrators.com*) are all examples of software metering packages. In addition, some security software packages—examples include Full Control (*www.bardon.com*), WinU (*www.bardon.com*), and CybraryN (*www.cybraryn.com*)—have metering as well as security capabilities. It may also be possible for local systems specialists to develop in-house methods for metering the use of software applications on a network.

FILTERING SOFTWARE

A hot-button issue in libraries, content-filtering software is designed to prevent users (especially children) from accessing objectionable (chiefly pornographic or violent) Websites. Filtering software works by blocking access to a predetermined list of Websites deemed objectionable (*www.playboy.com*, *www.penthouse.com*, and so on) and/or by blocking access to Websites that contain selected terms ("hot sex," "XXX," and so on). Besides blocking Websites, a number of filtering software packages have the added benefit of offering useful security and metering features. On the downside, filtering software is nowhere near 100 percent effective at blocking objectionable material and so may give parents, teachers, and other guardians of children a false sense of security. Another drawback is that filtering software can block sites that are either entirely unobjectionable (some filtering software blocked Websites that discussed Super Bowl XXX because the Websites contained the banned term *XXX*) or block sites that are deemed objectionable only for the ideas they espouse and not because of any pornographic or violent content. There are many brands of filtering software on the market. The *Yahoo!* "Filtering and Blocking" page (*dir.yahoo.com/Business_and_Economy/Companies/Computers/Software/Internet/Blocking_and_Filtering*) provides a long list of filtering software Websites.

Karen G. Schneider's *A Practical Guide to Internet Filters*[1] is a seminal work on the topic of Internet filtering and should be consulted by anyone who is considering—or is under pressure to consider—filters. For a staunchly pro-filtering point of view, visit David Burt's Filtering Facts Website (*www.filteringfacts.org*).

Somewhat similar to the practice of content filtering is the practice of blocking Websites based on their function. This chiefly involves blocking Websites (or parts of Websites) that offer chat, e-mail, and games. The purpose of blocking such sites is to prevent users from engaging in recreational or unscholarly activities at public-access work-stations intended for information retrieval. Though less controversial than filtering for content, blocking by function still raises strong feel-ings among its advocates (who see it as promoting the needs of those who want to use library computers for scholarly research) and its op-ponents (who see it as a miserable way to address what is, in fact, a shortage of public-access workstations). At the time of this writing, there are no software packages available for blocking by function, but a systems specialist may be able to use proxy-server technology to configure an in-house method of blocking by function. Dan Lester maintains an online list (*www.84.com/blacklist.htm*) of e-mail, chat, and game Websites that are blocked from the public-access comput-ers at his institution, the Albertson Library at Boise State University.

APPLICATION SOFTWARE

Except for the issue of Mac versus Wintel operating systems, users of public-access computers are likely to be little concerned with system software. Application software, on the other hand, is a matter of great importance to users. There are thousands of applications that could potentially be made available on public-access computers, so it is not possible to list, much less discuss, all of them here. Instead, this sec-tion deals with some considerations for selecting application software and discusses some general categories of application software.

CONSIDERATIONS FOR SELECTING SOFTWARE APPLICATIONS

While the following considerations may seem obvious, they are often not thought of when selecting new software. Thinking through po-tential problems early in the software acquisition process allows you to either address the problems ahead of time or, in serious cases, opt out of acquiring a software application that gives every indication of being more trouble than it is worth.

What effect will the application have?

Before acquiring and offering any software application, it is impor-tant to consider the effects it will have. Choosing, for example, to offer a sophisticated desktop-publishing software program on public-access workstations will or could:

- Please users who have been asking for this type of software.
- Attract new users to the computer lab and the library.
- Tie-up workstations for longer periods of time than do other applications.
- Increase the amount of printing and/or create a demand for color printing.
- Result in user requests for more sophisticated hardware (bigger monitors, better video cards, Zip drives for saving large files, etc.) to enhance the application.
- Require training staff to help users with desktop-publishing software.
- Result in users asking staff for help with complex editorial and layout questions.

The fact that offering a particular software application may produce some bad effects need not deter you from choosing to go forward with it; it is only important that you go forward prepared to deal with the bad as well as with the good.

Commitment to support the application

Just as choosing to add a journal to a library collection implies a long-term commitment to pay for and archive that journal, choosing a software application implies a commitment to support that software by:

- Providing public-access workstations with sufficient computing power to run the application.
- Providing any necessary peripheral hardware needed to support the application. (For example, providing a color printer to support a graphic-arts application.)
- Acquiring enough copies of, or licenses for, the software application to meet user demands.
- Updating the software as new releases become available.
- Providing help to users of the software.

As this suggests, acquiring and installing an application is only the beginning of the commitment you take on when you choose to offer an application on public-access computers.

User input

When it comes to applications, giving users what they want and need is an important goal. What is the use of providing, for example, map-making software if users really want a computer-aided drafting program? Why install Harvard Graphics presentation software if users overwhelmingly prefer PowerPoint? Why choose Microsoft Word when users really want WordPerfect? Getting user input does not necessarily lock you in to bowing to user demands in every case, but user input should factor into any final decision.

CATEGORIES OF SOFTWARE APPLICATIONS

Productivity software

Productivity software is a catchall term for word processors, presentation programs, and other applications used in business and education to produce specific final products—documents, presentations, spreadsheets, databases, and so on. If the raison d'être of your public-access computers is online searching and access to electronic resources, offering productivity software may be inappropriate. If offering productivity software is appropriate, such software can be acquired application by application or as suites (software packages that bundle together a number of productivity applications). Some of the more prominent productivity software suites are the Corel WordPerfect suite and the Microsoft Office suite. Acquiring software suites is less expensive than acquiring the same applications individually, but suites may include some applications that you will not want to offer on your public-access computers. It is also quite possible to offer productivity software on some computers while not offering it on others. Perhaps only three of twenty workstations will have PowerPoint. Or only the computers in the second-floor lab will have word processing while those on the first floor will not.

Web browsers

The two leading Web browsers are Netscape and Internet Explorer. Both are freeware, and, as far as the user interface goes, the two are so similar that the average person would not immediately notice any difference if one browser were switched for the other. With either browser, the version (release) of the software is more important than the brand. Whenever possible, install the most recent version of whichever browser you provide. Providing both browsers is an option, although this route means taking on the added burden of supporting two browsers.

There is also the option of using neither of the leading Web browsers and going with some other brand. While some third-party browsers (such as Opera) are touted as improvements over the two leading browsers, users' unfamiliarity with any browser other than Netscape or Internet Explorer could be a drawback. Another browser to be aware of is Lynx. A very early Web browser, Lynx displays only text, not images, but it has the advantage of working well with older, less powerful computers and slow modem connections. You can learn about different brands of Web browsers by visiting the *Yahoo!* Browser page (*dir.yahoo.com/Computers_and_Internet/Software/Internet/ World_Wide_Web/Browsers*).

Telnet applications

Telnet applications allow users to access telnet-based resources on the Internet, most notably online library catalogs. Telnet is also used to access remote mainframe computers for FTP, checking e-mail, and other purposes. Most often, telnet is used in conjunction with a Web browser, and there are many telnet applications that work well with Web browsers. Typing "telnet" in the search box at either *www.download.com* or *www.tucows.com* will produce long lists of telnet applications, most of them freeware.

Helper applications

Also known as *plugins*, helper applications are applications that work with a Web browser to extend the browser's capabilities. Most helper applications are available as freeware, although it is common for software makers to charge for the top-of-the-line version of a popular helper application.

There are scores of helper applications available. Arguably, the single most important helper application is Adobe Acrobat Reader (*www.adobe.com/prodindex/acrobat/readstep.html*), a widely available freeware application which allows users to read and print .pdf files. Because articles from many online journals are stored as .pdf files, Adobe Acrobat Reader is a must if users wish to access online journals.

There are a number of multimedia helper applications that allow browsers to access sound files (WAV, MIDI, RealAudio, MP3), movies (Quick Time, MPEG, AVI, VDOLive, RealVideo), animation (ShockWave, Flash), and more. While much Internet multimedia is entertainment oriented, it is increasingly used for scholarly purposes. For example, the Chemscape Chime helper application allows users to view models of chemical structures in a Web browser, while Techexplorer lets users view scientific and mathematical expressions coded in TeX format. There are also helper applications that allow users to view text written in non-western alphabets.

Because most helper applications are free, there is some temptation to load them on to workstations by the dozens. But for the sake of hard-drive space and staff sanity, you should set limits on which helper applications you provide. Some sources for learning more about helper applications include:

- Netscape Browser Plug-ins
  home.netscape.com/plugins/index.html

- BrowserWatch Plug-in Plaza
  browserwatch.internet.com/plug-in.html

- *Yahoo!* Plug-Ins
  dir.yahoo.com/Computers_and_Internet/Software/Internet/
  World_Wide_Web/Browsers/Plug_Ins/

Accessibility software

Along with the accessibility hardware discussed in Chapter 3, "Computer Hardware," accessibility software serves to maintain, increase, or improve the capabilities of a person with a disability. Examples of accessibility software include:

- Screen-magnification programs
- Screen-reading software that converts text and graphics to speech
- Voice-output software that scans text and converts it to speech
- Speaking Web browser software such as pwWebSpeak (*www. prodworks.com*)

See Chapter 3 for a list of Websites that provide information about accessibility software and hardware.

Specialty software

There is a universe of specialty software that you could make available to users. Whether or not you do depends on the mission of your institution. An art library might install sophisticated graphics software on its public-access computers. A technology-and-engineering library might install software for computer-aided design (CAD) or for writing computer programs. A community-college library might install software that supports adult literacy. What specialty software (if any) to install and how many workstations to install it on are, of course, local decisions. Your mission, the needs of your users, what software applications you can support, and what you can afford are all parts of the equation.

Focus On:

Lab or Library?

When public-access computers first sneaked through library doors in the form of online catalogs, their purpose was clearly related to the library's traditional mission. In fact librarians would often refer to OPACs as "computer card catalogs" or "online card catalogs," names which recognized the OPAC's place in the traditional library structure. But as dumb-terminal online catalogs turned into microcomputers, and as those microcomputers started to offer more than access to the local library catalog, the public-access computer's relationship to the traditional mission of the library became less clear. Put word processors on a library computer? What does word processing have to do with libraries? Or spreadsheets? Graphics programs? E-mail? Indeed, as library public-access computers offer more and more software applications, they tend to look more like computers found in straight computer labs than like the old online catalog.

There is nothing fundamentally wrong with having "computer lab" workstations in a library. Nor is there anything fundamentally wrong with keeping library computers configured (as much as possible) for research alone. And, to state the obvious, there is nothing fundamentally wrong with having some hybrid of the two. What is important is that the library is fully aware of what kind of public-access computers it has, that the library is willing and able to support the kind of public-access computers it has, and that the library's public-access computers support the mission of the library.

PURCHASING CONSIDERATIONS

Once you have settled on a particular software application, the main consideration is price. Shop around before buying, as the price for the same software can vary from vendor to vendor. Sometimes you can save money by buying directly from the software manufacturer or by buying via the Internet. Be sure to ask about any discounts for non-profit and educational institutions that might apply. As mentioned above, buying a software suite can reduce the cost per application. If you are planning to provide the same software application on more

---

Focus On:

Software as Commodity

When thought of as a commodity, software falls into one of three categories:

FREEWARE

Freeware, as the name implies, is software that anyone can use free of charge. While many freeware applications qualify as not much more than playthings (screen savers, antiquated computer games, and so on), and while some are merely scaled-down demonstration versions of proprietary software, there are a number of extremely popular and useful freeware applications. Prime examples include the Linux operating system, the Netscape Web browser, Adobe Acrobat Reader, and the many freeware media players available over the Internet. Most freeware applications require users to complete an online registration form before downloading the software.

SHAREWARE

Shareware is software that can be freely acquired for testing on the understanding that the tester will pay for the software if it proves satisfactory. Some shareware applications work on the honor system, while others are designed to stop working a set number of days after installation. As with freeware, some shareware applications are demonstration versions of proprietary software.

PROPRIETARY SOFTWARE

Proprietary software is commercially produced software that must be paid for in order to be used. Both proprietary software and shareware may be purchased under licenses that allow the software to be loaded on multiple workstations or served to multiple users over a network.

than one workstation, multi-user licenses or site licenses are normally the least costly option. Finally, make sure you acquire software from a reputable source—the last thing you want is to discover you have purchased pirated or defective software.

Before loading any software on a server or workstation, it is crucial that you are in compliance with whatever licensing restrictions apply. For example, the license for a piece of proprietary software may allow you to load it on only one workstation. Or it may allow you to load the software on multiple workstations but not on a network server. Software may also come with limits on the maximum number of simultaneous users. A piece of freeware may be free in an educational/non-profit setting but not free in a commercial setting, such as a corporate library. Using unlicensed software or failing to comply with licensing agreements can result in civil or even criminal penalties. Note also that users of public-access computers can violate software licenses by either loading software onto, or downloading software from, public-access workstations.

SOFTWARE FORMATS

Software typically either comes on disk or is downloaded over the Internet.

Disks

Proprietary software usually comes on disk. The more common format is CD-ROM disc, though 3.5" floppy diskettes are still used for smaller software applications. Some applications may require a disk (or set of disks) for each workstation, while other applications may provide only a single disk (or set of disks) that can be copied to multiple workstations. Disks may come with a registration number that must be entered when the software is loaded, and some disks have shrink-wrap licenses which go into effect once the seal on the disk has been broken. Once software has been loaded onto a workstation or server, it is vital to keep track of all disks and any accompanying documentation (including licensing agreements). Labeled file folders or pamphlet boxes are two good ways to store software disks and documentation. Be sure to keep with each disk (or set of disks) a record of which workstations and/or servers onto which the software has been loaded.

Downloadable software

Freeware and shareware are typically available for downloading from the Internet, and some proprietary software is available in this way as well. Before downloading and using any software, make sure you understand the licensing agreement and are prepared to comply with it. Just because an application is downloaded from the Internet does not mean it can be pirated with impunity.

Tip Sheet

Downloading Software

Downloading via the Internet is a popular way to try out and acquire software applications. Two popular and reputable Websites from which you can download a wide variety of applications are:

> TUCOWS
> *www.tucows.com*

and

> Download.com
> *www.download.com*

The above sites are not only good for downloading freeware, shareware, and demos, they are also good for discovering what applications are available. Going to either site and typing a key term into the search box ("browsers" for example) will pull up a long list of relevant software applications.

In most cases, when you download software applications from TUCOWS, Download.com, or any other Website, what you actually download is an executable (.exe) file that contains the compressed software application as well as a wizard program that automatically extracts and installs the application. When you begin to download an executable file of this type, you will be prompted to pick the directory to which you would like to save it. You can save the executable file to an existing directory (C:/temp is a good option) or create a new directory. Once you begin downloading an executable file, the process can last anywhere from a few seconds to a few hours depending on the size of the file and the speed of your Internet connection.

After the download has been completed, you need to locate the executable file in the directory you downloaded it to and then run it. To run an executable file either use your computer's Run function (found in the Start menu on Windows 95/98/NT) or double click on the file name. When the executable file begins to run, you will be prompted with on-screen instructions. Once the installation is complete, you may be prompted to restart your computer, a necessary step before running most downloaded applications.

Because downloading software from the Internet is one way to pick up computer viruses, make sure you download only from reputable Internet sites and/or that you run an up-to-date antivirus program on the software you download. The Websites of reputable software companies (Adobe, RealPlayer, Netscape, and so on) are safe places from which to download software, as are TUCOWS and Download.com.

Testing new software

Thoroughly testing new software is a must. Tests should be conducted either before the software is paid for or during a full-money-back-guarantee period agreed to by the software vendor. New software must be tested despite any and all assurances that testing is not necessary. Vendor phrases such as "fully compatible," "plug and play," "turn-key," and "run on any system" should be filed under "The Check is in the Mail" until the software has been tested and proven on the computer systems (network and workstations) on which it will *actually* run. Finally, software must be rigorously tested before it is made available to users. There are few things that will make you look worse than trumpeting some new software only to find that it crashes the system every time a user tries to run it.

While testing software is typically a function of the systems department, public service staff can (and should) be part of the process. The best kind of testing puts the software on the actual computers and/or network it will run on and subjects it to every eventuality that can be dreamed up. Depending on how the software will be used, questions you should keep in mind during testing include:

- Does the software install properly?
- Does it regularly crash or freeze?
- Does it conflict with other software already running on our workstations or network?
- Does it run well on our workstations?
- Does it run well on our network?
- Do *all* of its features work?
- Have we tested all features?
- Does it work when there are multiple users?
- Does it work for remote users?
- Does it print properly?
- Does it create any security holes in our workstations or network?
- How good is the support provided by the manufacturer?
- How good is the online help?
- How easy is it to use?
- Does it have a friendly user interface?
- Does it have good help screens?
- How good is the documentation?
- Does it do the job we acquired it to do?

ACCESS TO SOFTWARE: SERVERS AND HARD DRIVES

There are two choices for providing users with access to software applications: the software can be loaded onto a server that is networked to public-access workstations or it can be loaded onto the hard drives of one or more public-access workstations.

SERVERS

When software applications are loaded onto a server so they can be shared by workstations on a local area network (LAN), the server functions as a remote hard drive on which the applications are stored and run. One advantage of such a configuration is that an application needs to be loaded on only one computer (the server), making the chores of maintenance and updating easier while providing a high level of security for the software. Loading an application onto a server can also make it available from any workstation on the network rather than from specific workstations only and is helpful if you wish to take advantage of the cost savings that can result from software site licenses.

Some disadvantages of loading applications onto a server are that applications may run more slowly on a server than on a workstation hard drive and that some applications may not run on a server at all. Of course if there is no network and server already in place, you would need to take on the expense of installing and maintaining these items in order to serve applications.

WORKSTATION HARD DRIVES

The advantages and disadvantages of loading applications directly onto workstation hard drives are simply the flip side of the advantages and disadvantages of loading them onto a server. If the license does not allow an application to be loaded onto to a server, you have no choice except to load it onto a hard drive.

NOTE

1. Schneider, Karen G. 1997. *A Practical Guide to Internet Filters*. New York: Neal-Schuman Publishers.

5 CD-ROM

CD-ROM (Compact Disc-Read Only Memory) has proven to be one of the longest-lasting, most reliable, and most versatile storage-and-retrieval mediums in the history of computing. A CD-ROM disc holds 650MB of data, but unlike a floppy disk it cannot be written to without special equipment and, once written to, cannot be erased and written to again. CD-ROM discs have been used to store music, images, texts, software programs, and databases for such a long time that many wonder how much longer the CD-ROM format will remain vital. The larger-capacity DVD format is already challenging CD-ROM,[1] but the demise of the CD-ROM is still likely to be some years distant. Computer Economics, a research firm, predicted that 1999 will be the peak year for shipments of CD-ROM drives and that shipments of DVD and CD-RW (Compact Disc-Re Writeable) drives will continue to increase for at least the next five years.[2]

Even so, there are so many CD-ROMs—and so many CD-ROM players—that it is unlikely that computer users will abandon CD-ROMs with the speed with which they abandoned the 5.25" floppy disk. As a storage-and-retrieval medium, the CD-ROM disc has the advantage of being inexpensive yet capacious enough to store a significant amount of data, such as the contents of an entire book (or several books). CD-ROM discs can be rendered useless by scratching, bending, melting, and being jammed into the wrong drive, but all-in-all they are ruggedly durable. One major concern about CD-ROM is just how long data stored on a CD-ROM disc will remain stable and usable. While this question has yet to be definitively answered, current estimates are that CD-ROM data begins to degrade in 5 to 15 years—an eyeblink when compared to the many centuries that text will endure on properly stored acid-free paper.

It may be that CD-ROM will see its longest life as a storage-and-retrieval medium for monographs or monograph-like publications. It is quite common for science, math, and engineering books to come with an accompanying CD-ROM disc, and CD-ROM is a handy and inexpensive medium for many reference materials (study guides, dictionaries, directories, encyclopedias), multimedia publications that require little or no video, and small specialty databases that require only infrequent updates.

Where the use of CD-ROM has fallen away sharply is as a storage-and-retrieval medium for large bibliographic databases. Through the late 1980s and much of the 1990s, CD-ROMs were the favored medium for such large databases as *ERIC*, *Agricola*, *PsycLIT*, and the *MLA International Bibliography*. By the end of the 1990s, however, most libraries were accessing these and other large bibliographic databases via the World Wide Web rather than through CD-ROM discs.

Three Types of CD-ROM Discs

THE EVERYTHING-ON-THE-HARD-DRIVE DISC

This type of CD-ROM is designed to load all of its data and its client software (the software that runs the CD-ROM) onto the hard drive of a workstation (or server). Once the data and software are loaded, they can be accessed whether or not the CD-ROM is present in the CD-ROM drive. This type of CD-ROM is most often used to load proprietary software programs (word processors, utility programs, games, etc.) onto hard drives, but there are also some bibliographic and monographic CD-ROMs that work in this way.

THE CLICK-AND-RUN DISC

Because its client software goes to work as soon as the disc begins to run, this type of CD-ROM can be used without loading any software in advance. It is a simple matter to run this type of CD-ROM on virtually any workstation that has a CD-ROM drive, but the disc must be present in the CD-ROM drive the entire time the product is being used.

THE CLIENT-SOFTWARE DISC

This type of CD-ROM disc requires that its client-software be loaded onto a workstation's hard drive prior to running the CD-ROM disc. The client software is usually loaded by running an executable file (look for a filename followed by the file extension .exe) that is included on the CD-ROM disc. The executable file initiates a set-up procedure that writes the client software to the workstation's hard drive. Once the set-up procedure is complete, the disc must be present in the CD-ROM drive in order to use the product.

While having a physical CD-ROM on the premises can be a hedge against Internet disruptions (as well as a comfort to those who want something tangible in exchange for their collection-development dollars), when it comes to large databases, Web access has several advantages over CD-ROM:

Serving Large Databases: Web versus CD-ROM	
Web Access	**CD-ROM Access**
Large databases can be stored as single entities.	Large databases must be stored on multiple discs.
Lends itself to providing remote access.	Can be difficult to provide remote access.
Can be continuously updated.	Can be updated only periodically.
Potentially unlimited number of simultaneous users.	Limited number of simultaneous users.
Has the storage capacity to accommodate large numbers of full-text documents.	Lacks the storage capacity to accommodate large numbers of full-text documents.

CD-ROM HARDWARE

A CD-ROM drive is the hardware that spins the CD-ROM disc and reads the data on the disc with a laser beam. CD-ROM drive speed is indicated as 2×, 4×, 8×, and so on. The × in this equation stands for 150KB per second—the transfer speed of the original CD-ROM drives. Thus a 4× CD-ROM transfers data at 600KB per second, an 8× at 1200KB per second, and so on. At this time the fastest commercially available CD-ROM drives run at 32×, but top speeds go up every year. Faster CD-ROM drives are especially advantageous in networking scenarios where multiple users simultaneously access data from the same CD-ROM disc.

Relatively new on the market are CD-R (Compact Disc-Readable) and CD-RW (Compact Disc-Re Writeable) drives and discs. A CD-R drive can write to a CD-R disc one time only. A CD-RW drive can write to a CD-RW disc up to 1,000 times. One very practical use of CD-R and CD-RW technology is creating back-ups of computer hard drives. CD-RW discs cannot be read by standard CD-ROM drives because the discs have a lower reflectivity; however, CD-RW drives can read regular CD-ROM discs.

SINGLE CD-ROM DRIVE

The most common configuration for CD-ROM hardware is a single CD-ROM drive built into a microcomputer in much the same manner as a 3.5" floppy disk drive. Older microcomputers may have an external CD-ROM drive that attaches to the microcomputer via a cable.

DAISY-CHAINED CD-ROM DRIVES

Daisy chaining involves connecting two or more CD-ROM drives to a microcomputer via cables. Each CD-ROM drive in a daisy chain is designated by a unique drive letter (D:, E:, F:, etc.). If there is a problem with one drive in the daisy chain, the whole chain will go down.

CD-ROM DISC CHANGER

A CD-ROM disc changer is a single CD-ROM drive that holds a small number of discs (typically six to twelve). Each time a user accesses a disc, the changer must physically move the requested disc into playing position. This is a mechanical process which slows down access to data. Disc changers are often used with CD-ROM products that span multiple discs, as putting all the discs in a single changer makes access easier while reducing the amount of (potentially damaging) handling the discs must endure.

CD-ROM JUKEBOX

A typical CD-ROM jukebox holds anywhere from twenty to several hundred CD-ROM discs and has from six to twelve CD-ROM drives—more drives than a CD-ROM changer but fewer than a CD-ROM tower. When a user accesses a disc via a jukebox, the jukebox must physically place the disc in one of its drives, a process that both slows down access and prevents multiple users from accessing the same disc simultaneously. Though access via a CD-ROM jukebox is slower than access via a CD-ROM tower, a jukebox can store and serve many more CD-ROM discs for much lower cost than a tower.

CD-ROM TOWER

A CD-ROM tower may contain several dozen CD-ROM drives. Because there is one disc in each drive, there is no waiting while a disc is mechanically placed in a drive. Also, multiple users can access a single disc simultaneously. CD-ROM towers are an expensive means of serving very large numbers of discs. The middle of 1999 saw the shipping of the first DVD towers; these towers handle DVD discs exactly as CD-ROM towers handle CD-ROM discs.

CD-ROM Licensing Agreements

CD-ROM licensing agreements may be either formal, signed agreements or shrink-wrap agreements that go into effect as soon as you break the seal on the CD-ROM package.[3] Read the CD-ROM licensing agreement and be sure you are not in violation of it before doing any of the following:

* Copying any part of a CD-ROM (including its client software) to any hard drive or disk.

* Providing access to a CD-ROM on more than one workstation.

* Networking a CD-ROM in any way.

* Providing remote access to a CD-ROM.

CD-ROM SERVERS

A CD-ROM server caches (copies) CD-ROMs to its hard drive and serves them over a network. Because they do not use CD-ROM drives and discs to serve data to users, CD-ROM servers are fast and, like CD-ROM towers, allow multiple users to access a single disc simultaneously. Large CD-ROM servers have capacities that can reach nearly 300 CD-ROMs, and some can serve both CD-ROM and DVD discs.

CD-ROM jukeboxes, towers, and servers all reduce the physical handling of CD-ROM discs, virtually eliminate theft of discs, and do away with the need to check out CD-ROMs to users. They make it possible for every workstation on the network to be a CD-ROM workstation, and they open up the possibility of serving CD-ROMs to remote users.

Unless your library has an unusually small collection of CD-ROMs, or can afford to spend a great deal of money on CD-ROM hardware, it is unlikely that you can afford to serve all of your CD-ROM discs via a CD-ROM jukebox, tower, or server. While it is, of course, possible to switch CD-ROM discs in and out of a jukebox or tower, few libraries want to put themselves in the position of constantly switching discs to satisfy user demands. Therefore, each library must carefully select which CD-ROM discs are so important, or in such demand, that they deserve a spot in tower, jukebox, or server; also, each library must periodically review and re-evaluate their selections. Finally, the library must provide users with a way to access those CD-ROMs that are not stored in jukebox, tower, or server.

PROVIDING ACCESS TO CD-ROMS

Assuming that CD-ROM (or its heir-apparent, DVD) is going to be around for a while, it is important to be aware of the challenges of providing access to CD-ROMs. CD-ROMs are typically accessed from a hard drive, from a designated CD-ROM workstation, or via a networked device (CD-ROM jukebox, tower, or server).

CD-ROMS ACCESSED FROM HARD DRIVE

It may be possible to cache (copy) the entire contents of a CD-ROM disc on a hard drive. Caching a CD-ROM disc on a hard drive protects the disc from theft and damage, and retrieval of data from a hard drive is often faster than if the data on the disc were served in some other way. Before a CD-ROM can be cached on a hard drive, you will have to determine if the CD-ROM is capable of being cached. This will likely involve individually testing each CD-ROM disc you wish to cache. Also make sure that the CD-ROM's licensing agreement allows for caching to a hard drive. A CD-ROM can be cached to a networked hard drive, facilitating access across a local area network or via remote connections.

CD-ROMS ACCESSED FROM DESIGNATED WORKSTATIONS

A designated CD-ROM workstation is a microcomputer equipped with the necessary CD-ROM drives and client software to run one or more CD-ROM discs. Under this scenario users must go to a specific workstation (or workstations) to access specific CD-ROM discs.

Locked-down discs

One designated-workstation scenario is to use commercially available CD-ROM drive locks to lock discs in place on designated CD-ROM workstations. You may provide access to either one disc per workstation or to several discs per workstation if the workstation has daisy-chained CD-ROM drives or a CD-ROM changer. Locking CD-ROM discs into drives protects the discs but means that there is only one point of access to each CD-ROM disc (unless you acquire multiple copies of a disc).

Check-out discs

An alternative designated-workstation scenario is to allow users to check out discs and put them into the CD-ROM drives of any one of several designated workstations. A disc check-out system may be a formal one in which users go to a circulation desk and present their library cards, or it may be a more informal system where users obtain discs from a reference or help desk (possibly in exchange for a driver's license or student ID). In either case, check out normally allows for in-house use only. Even with an in-house limitation, allowing users to check out discs opens up the possibility of theft[4] or damage. The advantage of a check-out system is that it makes it easy to provide multiple points of access for each disc. For example, if you set up ten workstations to run three popular CD-ROMs (let's say, *Netter's Anatomy on CD-ROM*, *College Catalogs on CD-ROM*, and the *Agricola* database), a user who checks out the *Agricola* disc has ten access points to choose from rather than the one that would be available if the *Agricola* disc were locked into a single drive on a single workstation.

CD-ROMS ACCESSED VIA A NETWORKED DEVICE

CD-ROM jukeboxes, towers, and servers are devices intended to be networked to a local area network (LAN). They can be configured to provide access to users on a LAN as well as to remote users who either dial in to the LAN via modem or access it via the Internet. Single CD-ROM drives, daisy-chained CD-ROM drives, and CD-ROM disc changers are normally not networked, though it is possible to do so under advanced network software such as Windows NT.

Before networking any CD-ROM, it is crucial to make certain that it is, in fact, technologically possible to network the CD-ROM and to be certain that the license agreement allows networking. If the license does not allows networking, you will either have to negotiate a new license agreement with the CD-ROM vendor (always get new agreements in writing) or forego networking the CD-ROM altogether. Note that some licensing agreements allow networking within a single building (or campus) but do not allow access by remote users. If remote access is allowed under the license agreement, it is likely that it requires you to have in place some system of restricting access to authorized users only. Finally, license agreements may limit the number of simultaneous users.

To serve a CD-ROM disc to remote-access users it is necessary to 1) serve the CD-ROM's client software to the remote-access user and 2) emulate a local CD-ROM interface. Both of these problems can be difficult to overcome, but there are some effective software/hardware solutions on the market.[5] One popular solution is Citrix WinFrame, a software product that allows users to access networked CD-ROM products through their Web browsers. Microtest's DiscPort Enterprise Servers offers yet another solution. The hardware, software, and labor required to provide remote-access to CD-ROMs can be quite expensive and should be figured into the cost of any CD-ROM you intend to network. To aid in determining how to choose a CD-ROM network, a checklist is given in Figure 5–1. In cases where there is both a

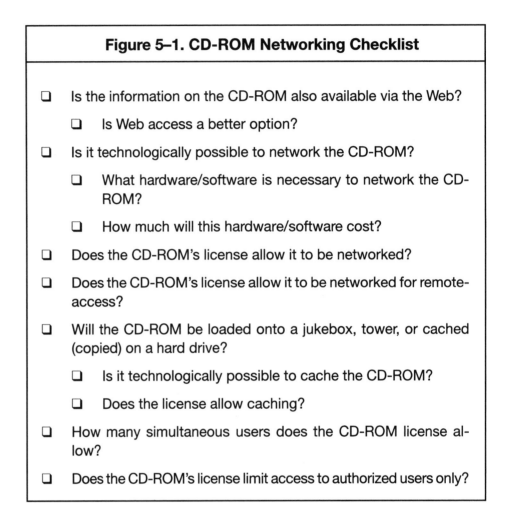

Figure 5–1. CD-ROM Networking Checklist

❑ Is the information on the CD-ROM also available via the Web?

  ❑ Is Web access a better option?

❑ Is it technologically possible to network the CD-ROM?

  ❑ What hardware/software is necessary to network the CD-ROM?

  ❑ How much will this hardware/software cost?

❑ Does the CD-ROM's license allow it to be networked?

❑ Does the CD-ROM's license allow it to be networked for remote-access?

❑ Will the CD-ROM be loaded onto a jukebox, tower, or cached (copied) on a hard drive?

  ❑ Is it technologically possible to cache the CD-ROM?

  ❑ Does the license allow caching?

❑ How many simultaneous users does the CD-ROM license allow?

❑ Does the CD-ROM's license limit access to authorized users only?

Web-based and a CD-ROM version of a particular information resource, it is, in the end, frequently less costly to go with the Web-version even if its sticker price is higher than that of the CD-ROM version.

FULL-TEXT CD-ROM SETS

Another type of CD-ROM product often found in libraries and learning centers is the full-text CD-ROM set. Most often these sets consist of bibliographic software along with a set of CD-ROMs that contain full-text documents. Users search the bibliographic software and retrieve citations that direct them to specific CD-ROM discs on which they will find the full text of the cited documents. Because the number of full-text discs in even a small CD-ROM set is too large to serve over a CD-ROM jukebox, tower, or server,[6] and because full-text CD-ROM sets are neither designed nor licensed for remote access, access to the discs must take some other form.

Typically, users either check out the full-text discs as they need them or else locate the full-text discs they need in self-service racks or cabinets. The advantage of check out is that it curtails theft, but check out is labor intensive for library staff and frustrating to users. Self-service is less labor intensive and more convenient, but it leads to stolen and misplaced discs. One factor that curtails theft is that discs from most full-text CD-ROM sets can be read only with the vendor's proprietary software—users may steal the discs, but they soon learn they cannot access the documents on them.

The discs from full-text CD-ROM sets are sometimes stored in CD-ROM caddies. The entire caddy, with the CD-ROM inside, is inserted into the CD-ROM drive, thereby protecting the discs from the hazards of frequent handling. The downsides of caddies are that caddies themselves are expensive and CD-ROM drives which accept caddies can be hard to come by and are more expensive than regular CD-ROM drives.

CIRCULATING CD-ROMS

If your library's circulating collection includes any current science or technology books, you are checking out CD-ROMs whether you realize it or not. As for CD-ROMs that do not come as supplements to printed books, it is important to carefully consider the pluses and minuses of circulating them without falling into the "We don't do that because we've never done that" trap. One approach is to treat CD-ROMs much as books are treated:

- Reference CD-ROMs, like reference books, stay in the library.

- Extremely rare or valuable CD-ROMs, like rare or valuable books, stay in the library.
- High-use CD-ROMs, like high-use books, are treated as reserve materials which leave the library for either a short time or not at all.
- Low-use CD-ROMs, like books in the stacks, can circulate.

One argument in favor of circulating at least some selected CD-ROMs is that many people now have CD-ROM players in their homes and are quite accustomed to loading and using CD-ROMs without assistance. Also, if the library allows CD-ROMs to circulate, the library is less obligated to provide users with workstations configured to run those CD-ROMs. Before circulating any CD-ROM, however, be certain that circulating it (which may result in borrowers downloading data or software from the CD-ROM to their hard drives) does not violate the license agreement.

PERSONAL CD-ROMS IN THE LIBRARY

"Can I run my CD-ROM on your computers?" is a question heard by library staff more and more often. While allowing users to run their own CD-ROMs is a nice service, running CD-ROMs often requires access to a workstation's hard drive, opening the door to hacking and computer viruses. One possible solution is to designate an older, non-networked computer as the workstation on which users may run their personal CD-ROMs. That way, if the workstation is hacked or infected with a virus, the loss is minimal and no other workstations are affected. Users who copy CD-ROM client software onto a library computer in order to run their own CD-ROMs may be violating copyright. Regularly cleaning user-installed client software off library workstations should keep the library out of copyright trouble and will also keep workstation hard drives from filling up with unnecessary programs.

NOTES

1. The complete full-text *National Geographic*, which fills over 30 CD-ROMs, will fit on a single DVD disc.
2. "CD-ROM Drive Shipments Are Expected to Peak This Year, Says Research Firm Computer Economics." 1999. *Computers in Libraries*. 6 (June): 60.
3. There is still some debate over the legality of shrink-wrap licensing agreements. But unless you are ready to take it all the way to the Supreme Court, for the time being it is best to abide by shrink-wrap licensing agreements. If you cannot comply with the conditions of a shrink-wrap (or any other) licensing agreement, contact the vendor of the product and let them know what it is about the agreement that you do not like. The vendor may very well write you a new agreement in order to keep your business; if not, you have lost nothing and possibly planted a seed of change in the vendor's mind.
4. The 3M Corporation manufactures a special Tattle Tape™ just for CD-ROM and DVD discs (*www.mmm.com/library/prod_mp_03.html*).
5. A good source for information on, and reviews of, the latest hardware and software for networking CD-ROMs and DVDs is the magazine *E Media Professional*.
6. It is quite likely that full-text CD-ROM sets will soon be replaced by full-text DVD sets for the simple reason that DVD sets will require many fewer discs.

6 PRINTING

Despite all the talk about a fully wired, paperless society, anyone who works with public-access computers knows that users still want paper copies of the documents they have created and print outs of the information they have looked up. Indeed, if a user is heading to the stacks to track down the full text of a few dozen citations just retrieved from a bibliographic database, having those citations in anything other than paper form is useless. Printing, it seems, is going to be with us for some time to come.

PRINTER ESSENTIALS

Familiarity with the following terms will help you understand how printers work and what makes one printer superior to another.

BUFFER

A printer buffer holds print jobs in memory while the jobs are either printing or waiting to print. Buffers allow computers to send an entire print job to a printer all at once instead of a page at a time. (See RAM below.)

DPI

DPI (dots per inch) is a measure of printing quality. The more DPI, the better the final product will look. It is common for newer printers to be rated at 600 DPI or higher.

DRIVER

A printer driver is a software program that converts a print job sent from a computer into a format the printer can understand. Printer drivers come with new printers (usually on CD-ROM discs) and must be loaded onto the microcomputer in order to print. If you do not have a driver for a particular printer, you can usually download the driver for free from the Website of the company that manufactures the printer.

DUTY CYCLE

A printer's duty cycle is the number of pages per month (PPM) the printer is rated to print under normal conditions. Thus a printer with a duty cycle of 7,000 PPM is rated for heavier use than a printer with a duty cycle of 5,000 PPM.

LETTER QUALITY

The term *letter quality* describes printing that is equal in quality to that produced by a typewriter. As a standard, letter quality is somewhat outdated as many laser printers now print text that is better than that produced on a typewriter. The terms *near letter quality* (NLQ) and *draft quality* describe printing that is inferior to letter quality.

RAM

The more RAM (random access memory) a printer has, the larger its buffer. A large buffer is necessary for handling multiple print jobs and printing complex images.

SPEED

Printer speed is measured in either CPS (characters per second), LPM (lines per minute), or PPM (pages per minute). Printer speed is particularly important when networking several workstations to a single printer.

TYPES OF PRINTERS

All of the following types of printers are routinely used in public-access computer settings. Other types of printers, such as large-format printers and line printers, are so rarely, if ever, used in public-access settings as to be inconsequential.

DOT-MATRIX PRINTERS

Dot-matrix printers employ hammers and an inked ribbon to form images composed of tiny dots. The more pins a dot-matrix printer has, the better the quality of its printing. A 24–pin dot-matrix printer can produce letter-quality printing. The speeds of dot-matrix printers vary from 200 to 400 characters per second. Dot-matrix printers often use tractor feeds to print onto continuous sheets of paper, though some can print onto plain paper as well. Disadvantages of dot-matrix printers are that they are noisier than ink-jet and laser printers, can print only a limited number of fonts, and cannot print in color.

INK-JET PRINTERS

Ink-jet printers print text and graphics by squirting tiny droplets of ink onto sheets of paper. Ink-jet printers are popular because they are inexpensive, quiet, and produce good results, though in general the quality of ink-jet printing is not as good as that of laser printers. Many ink-jet printers can print in color. Less expensive color ink-jet printers use three ink colors, which results in muddy blacks. Higher-end ink-jet printers use pure black ink as their fourth color and so produce high-quality black text and images. Common ink-jet printers can print black-only pages at rates of from five to ten PPM, while color printing is less than half as fast. One thing to watch for when acquiring ink-jet printers is the cost of the ink cartridges. The cartridges used by some low-end ink-jet printers are so expensive that it is ultimately less costly to acquire a more expensive printer that uses less-expensive cartridges.

LASER PRINTERS

Laser printers print an entire page at one time. In a laser printer, a laser paints an image of a page onto an electromagnetic drum, toner adheres to the image, and the toner is then transferred and fused onto paper. Desktop laser printers use plain paper and print at speeds ranging from four to over thirty pages per minute. The print quality of even low-end laser printers is superior to all but the best ink-jet printers, and the print quality of high-end laser printers is unbeatable. Another advantage of laser printers is that some of the newer models can print on both sides of a page, which reduces paper consumption. Color laser printers are more expensive and slower than black-and-white laser printers, but the quality of their printing is outstanding and prices on color laser printers have been dropping in the last few years.

NETWORKED VERSUS NON-NETWORKED PRINTERS

The old model for printers in libraries was to have one printer connected to one computer workstation or, in some cases, one printer shared by two workstations with a manually operated data switch for connecting the printer to whichever workstation needed to print. Such arrangements eat up a lot of desktop space and are a supply and maintenance headache. The new model is to have many workstations networked to a single printer (which is almost always a laser printer). There are several advantages to this new model. Network printers:

- Save desktop space.
- Reduce maintenance costs.
- Simplify restocking paper and changing toner cartridges.
- Make it more affordable to provide users with high-quality printers.

- Permit the rerouting of print jobs when one printer goes down.
- Lend themselves to pay-for-print systems.

The big question with networked printers is, "How many workstations can you network to one printer?" This is a big question because there are, obviously, economic incentives to network as many workstations as possible to a single printer. Typically, a large-volume laser printer can handle from 20 to 40 workstations; however, the following factors should be considered when deciding how many workstations can, or should, be networked to one printer:

NETWORK LIMITATIONS

The capacity or configuration of your network may limit the number of workstations that can be connected to any one printer. Your systems department should be able to provide information on any such limitations. Also note that a printer network card may be required to network a printer and that such cards can cost several hundred dollars each.

DEMAND FOR PRINTING

High demand for printing will reduce the number of workstations you can network to one printer. Say you have one printer and twenty public-access workstations. If that printer has a duty cycle of 7,000 pages per month but the users of your twenty workstations routinely print over 14,000 pages per month, then you should acquire two printers and network ten workstations to each. Though acquiring two printers doubles the initial cost, in the long run the money saved on service calls, parts, and replacing prematurely worn-out printers will make the initial outlay worthwhile.

PRINTER CAPABILITIES

Fast printers with plenty of memory and the capacity to hold multiple reams of paper can support more workstations than slow, low-memory, low-capacity printers.

WAITING AND WALKING

How long should users have to wait for their print jobs and how far should they have to walk to retrieve them? If a large number of busy workstations are networked to a single printer, the waiting time can be significant. If workstations scattered around a building are networked to a central printer, the distance from workstation to printer can be a burden—especially for users with mobility problems.

PRINTER MAINTENANCE AND SERVICE

Even if you have a large systems department at your library, chances are there is no one in-house who can service the mechanical workings of a printer—especially a laser printer. Since almost any breakdown more complicated than a paper jam requires an outside service technician, a good printer-service contract is a necessity. Features to look for in a printer-service contract include routine maintenance visits, a minimum response time in the event of a breakdown, and the use of a loaner printer when a printer has to go into the shop. Be aware that using printers in excess of their duty cycles may void both service contracts and warranties.

Even with a service contract, you may need to do routine printer maintenance in house. Be sure that whoever does routine maintenance knows what they are doing and has read the printer manuals. Laser printers, for example, have delicate wires inside that, if bent or broken, will put the printer out commission. A hand vacuum is useful for keeping the insides of printers clean and for sucking up spilled toner.

PAPER

Paper is expensive. One way to keep down the cost of paper is to buy as much of it as you can at one time. Just as buying paper by the box is cheaper than buying it by the ream, buying one hundred boxes of paper at one time is cheaper than buying five. Besides being expensive, paper is also heavy and bulky, so before you pick up the telephone and order 100 boxes of paper, you will need a place to store it. That storage area must be large enough to store all the paper you order (100 boxes of paper, tightly packed, takes up about 150 cubic feet of space). The storage area will need to be locked or otherwise inaccessible to the public—leaving unsecured boxes or reams of paper in public areas is an invitation for theft. Ideally, the storage area should be on the first floor, as hoisting large loads of paper absolutely destroys passenger elevators and can wear out all but the most robust freight elevators. Whatever floor the storage room is on, get a qualified engineer to determine how much weight the floor can support before you start packing in large loads of paper. Finally, when you order a large load of paper, make sure you specify inside delivery from the freighter; otherwise, you may find yourself with several tons of paper on the loading dock and no way to move it to the storage area.

Once paper is in the storage area, it still needs to make its way to the printers. The duty of restocking printers with paper should be part of either opening or closing routines and can also be assigned on an as-needed basis. If staff need to move more than a few reams of paper from the storage area to the printers, they will need a hand truck or dolly. Anyone who must lift an entire box of paper for any reason should be trained in how to lift and supplied with a lifting belt. Unless the paper storage area is very close to the printers, it is a good idea to have a staging area where you can keep a box or more of paper on hand for quick restocking. The staging area might be behind the service desk or in a nearby office. Printer stands with locking doors and shelves are ideal for conveniently storing a few dozen reams of paper.

After it has made its trip through the printer, a lot of paper gets left behind. Recycling bins are better than trash bins for handling used paper. For recycling to work, there must be a recycling bin near every printer. In addition, somebody has to collect the paper and haul it to a recycling center. Local recycling offices, whether civic or campus, may be able to help coordinate the collection of used paper. Instead of trashing the empty boxes that paper comes in, offer them to users and staff—they make great moving and mailing boxes and are great for storing books awaiting the library's semi-annual book sale.

TONER AND INK CARTRIDGES

Not as bulky or heavy as paper, toner and ink cartridges still need to be stored in a secure area. Some points about toner and ink cartridges:

- As mentioned above, the cost of cartridges should be considered when purchasing a printer. Expensive cartridges can make a bargain printer no bargain.
- As printers get older, cartridges can become so expensive or hard to find that it is better to replace the printer than to try eking a few more years out of it.
- Low-capacity cartridges are a problem as they need to be changed constantly and are always running out in the middle of a user's print job.
- For color ink-jet printers that use a separate cartridge for black ink, be sure that you can change the black cartridge without having to replace the color cartridges as well.
- Be sure cartridges are installed properly and that everyone on the staff closely follows the installation instructions that come

Tip Sheet

Printing From the Web

Printing from the Web presents two challenges: printing selected parts of a Web page and printing Web pages that use white text.

SELECTING PARTS OF WEB PAGES

Because a single Web page can be the equivalent of scores of printed pages, being able to select and print only that part of a Web page that is wanted saves a lot of paper and toner. Selecting parts of Web pages is easy with recent versions of Internet Explorer. Use the mouse to highlight the text and images you wish to print and then select from the toolbar menu: **File, Print, Selection, OK**. Printing selected pages with Netscape is a bit more complicated since Netscape (at least up to version 4.5) does not allow you to use the mouse to select for printing. Instead, choose **File, Print Preview**. When the preview pages load, scan through them and take note of the numbers of the pages you wish to print. Click **Close**, then choose **File, Print, Pages** and enter the number of the page or pages you wish to print. Click **OK**.

WHITE TEXT

Some Web pages use white or very light text against a dark background, and very often such pages print out blank. In Netscape you can overcome this problem by using the **Color** settings under **Edit, Preferences** to force the Web page to use a white background and black text. With Internet Explorer you can do the same thing by using the **Colors** settings found under **View, Options, General**. Yet another option for any browser is to highlight and copy the text you wish to print, paste it into a word processor, and print from there.

with the cartridges. Improperly installed cartridges either do not work or work poorly. They can also damage printers.

- Toner cartridges for laser printers should be recycled. Purchasing recycled toner cartridges is less expensive than buying new ones, but some recycled cartridges perform so poorly that they end up costing more than the new ones. You may need to shop around to find the brand of recycled toner cartridge that works best in your printers.
- When a laser printer's "low toner" light comes on, removing the cartridge and shaking it a few times will usually extend the life of the cartridge.

PAY TO PRINT

In the days when printing from public-access computers meant a dot-matrix printer cranking out a list of citations and abstracts from a bibliographic database, the cost of printing was not a terrible burden. Today, when public-access printing means laser printers churning out term papers, full-text articles, and huge Web documents, the cost of printing has become more than most libraries can bear. This is why pay-to-print systems are becoming increasingly common in libraries and other public-access computer facilities.

The arguments against charging for printing are that systems to charge for printing are burdensome to both staff and users as well as expensive to implement and maintain. In addition, paying for printing can be such a financial burden to some users as to virtually cut off their access information. These are strong and compelling arguments, and they must be considered before jumping on the pay-to-print bandwagon. On the other hand, there are strong arguments in favor of charging for printing:

- Free printing is not, and never has been, free. Someone (the library, the city, the school) has always had to pay for it.
- The money saved by charging for printing can be used to acquire other resources, such as new workstations, software, books, and journals.
- Free printing encourages waste, as when users print out five-hundred-page computer-game manuals only to leave behind all but the three pages they actually wanted.
- Free printing encourages abuse, as when someone prints out several dozen copies of a resume in order to avoid the cost of photocopying.
- Because of all the full-text articles available online, printing has become more like photocopying, a service for which libraries have always charged.
- Charging for printing not only reduces the consumption of paper and toner, it also saves wear and tear on the printers.
- Charging even a few pennies per page will eliminate wasteful and profligate printing. *Any* pay-to-print system, even those that are not 100 percent effective, will send the amount of printing plunging.

If your library chooses to charge for printing, it is a decision that must be supported at the highest levels. Library administration and governing boards must endorse the change and be prepared to stand behind the library staff who are charged with effecting the change.

PAY-TO-PRINT SYSTEMS

There are really two ways to configure a pay-to-print system: human mediated and automated.

Human-mediated systems

In a human-mediated pay-to-print system, all print jobs go to printers located behind one or more service desks. When users want their printouts they must go to the service desk where a staff member retrieves their print job and collects payment. The advantage of this system is that it is relatively easy to set up and requires little or no initial outlay for software and equipment. The disadvantages, though, are significant:

- Every service desk with a printer must be constantly staffed. There must be a cash register and/or a copy-card reader at every such desk. The potential for fraud, as well as the potential accounting headaches, are both considerable.
- Many printouts will never be picked up. Users will simply abandon their printouts when they go to the desk and learn that they must pay for them.
- Keeping individual print jobs separate will be a constant chore, as will sorting through a pile of jobs to find the one that is wanted.

In practice, human-mediated systems will work only in small libraries with low volumes of printing. Some smaller libraries use honor systems where users pay for what they have printed after they have finished printing. Not all users pay, of course, but honor systems can reduce the amount of printing and recoup at least part of the library's printing costs. A tactic that works for non-networked printers is for the library to provide printers and toner but not to provide paper. Users can either bring their own paper or purchase small amounts from the library.

Automated systems[1]

By far, most libraries that charge for printing use automated systems. Such systems require: 1) a software package that controls printing and sets prices for each print job and 2) a copy-card reader and/or a coin box for each printer. Most systems also require that one microcomputer be dedicated to act as a server for each printer (though very often older, low-end microcomputers can fill this role just fine). Though the initial outlay for software and hardware can be considerable, the savings realized by an automated pay-to-print system can cover the cost of the system in a short time. Because there is no point in charging for printing if it will not produce substantial savings, you should do a cost-benefits analysis to determine if a pay-for-print system is

---

Figure 6–1: Desirable Features in Automated Pay-to-Print Systems

- Provides a friendly, easy-to-understand user interface.

- Tells users what their print job will cost before they send it to the printer and tells them again before they pay for it.

- Gives users several opportunities to cancel a print job prior to paying.

- Automatically names each print job but also gives users the option of naming print jobs themselves.

- Gives users the option of password-protecting print jobs so they cannot be printed or deleted by someone else.

- Allows users to pay for and print several print jobs at once.

- Is capable of working with the library's existing copy cards so that users do not need one card for photocopies and another for printing.

- Allows users to pay with either a copy card or with coins and bills.

- Automatically purges old print jobs after a period of time (two hours, twelve hours, etc.) determined by the library.

- Allows staff to override the system in case a job must be printed free of charge.

- Allows system administrators to easily change the amount charged for each printed page.

- Keeps good records of the number of pages printed, including time and date of printing.

- Other libraries that use the system recommend it.

- System vendor provides good technical support.

---

worthwhile. Be sure to include in your analysis the savings that will result from reduced printer maintenance and extended printer life. For small libraries, automated pay-to-print systems may never be cost effective. Figure 6–1 lists desirable features in automated pay-to-print systems.

Any automated pay-to-print system must be rigorously tested on your network and workstations to make sure that it actually works. When you bring up the system, it is a good idea to have a one month "free printing" period during which the system is in place but users are not actually charged for copies. This gives users a chance to accustom themselves to the system as well as to the idea that printing will no longer be free. During the first week or so of the test period, and again during the first week of the actual implementation, plan on scheduling extra staff to show users how the system works. The test period will also give public-service and systems staff a chance to get used to the system and work out the inevitable bugs without, at the same time, having to deal with unhappy users who want their money back.

Vendors

The following list includes major vendors of software and/or hardware for automated pay-to-print systems. The list of these companies is not intended as an endorsement of their products.

ITC Systems
www.itcsystems.com

OCS (Output Control Software)
www.vasinc.com/print.htm

pcounter
www.andtechnologies.com

SoftwareMetrics
www.metrics.com

UniPrint
www.uniprint.co.nz

Vendaprint
www.copicard.com

Preparing Users for Pay to Print

If your library has always offered free printing, you will need to spend some time and effort preparing users for the conversion. Most users will not like the change, and some will be outraged by it. Go in expecting such reactions and be prepared to accept the fact that nothing you can do will win over everyone.

The first step is to announce the change well in advance. Announce it via many media and announce it over and over again. Long (months) before the change takes place, announce it in newsletters, on Web pages, in handouts, at meetings with library users, on posters—in any way you can imagine. Keep on announcing the change over and over again. Your announcements can include justifications for the switch to a pay-to-print system, though do not expect everyone to be swayed by your persuasive arguments.

Displays that announce the change and illustrate the need for it are a good idea. You could make a display out of paper boxes representing the amount of paper the library uses in one week. Be sure the display informs users how much this amount of paper costs. Similarly, empty toner boxes can be used to illustrate the amount of toner used and its cost. Displaying the amount of paper that goes to the recycler in one week can also make a vivid point. Another option is to make a wall-sized chart illustrating what could be acquired with the money the library spends each year on "free" printing: *X* number of books, *X* number of journal subscriptions, *X* number of computer workstations, and so on. For a good example of a library pay-to-print publicity campaign, see the Duke University Medical Center Library's online poster session, "When It's Not Free Anymore: Promoting the Unpopular" (*www2.mc.duke.edu/misc/MLA/webposter*).

Alternatives

If completely eliminating free printing is unacceptable, one alternative is to charge for printing on laser printers but to provide free printing on dot-matrix printers. With a copy-card system, it may be possible to give users a certain amount of printing credit each year. Remember, though, that if you are using the same copy card for both printing and photocopying, giving printing credit is the same as giving photocopying credit.

Tricks that make printing more efficient—printing citations versus printing abstracts, marking items for printing versus printing one page at a time, printing only selected pages instead of an entire document—are especially important to users in a pay-to-print setting. Informing users about their printing options will help reduce complaints and make the burden of paying to print easier for users to bear.

While users always have the option of writing things down instead of printing, saving to disk is a more popular and practical option. You should strongly promote saving to disk and provide users with instructions on how to save documents to disk as well as on how to access saved documents from home and office computers. If you charge for printing, having diskettes available on the premises is a must. Diskettes can be sold from vending machines or at a service desk. Giving away free diskettes is not beyond the realm of possibility, though there should be a limit on how many free diskettes one user may have.

NOTE

1. For more information on automated printing systems, see Vidmar, Dale J., Marshall A. Berger, and Connie J. Anderson. 1998. "Fee or free? Printing from Public Workstations in the Library." *Computers in Libraries*. 5 (May): 26–30.

7 WORKING WITH THE SYSTEMS DEPARTMENT

"We have met the enemy, and he is us."
—*Walt Kelly's* Pogo

It is all too easy for the relationship between public-service and systems departments to turn adversarial.[1] To those in public service, the systems department can seem like a tribe of technogeeks whose chief occupation is saying "No" to all requests sent their way. To the systems department, public-service staff can seem like a band of technophobes whose chief pastime is making one impossible demand after another. When such an adversarial relationship exists, everybody (including library users) suffers. One of the most important jobs for the manager of public-access computers, therefore, is to establish and maintain the best possible relationship between the public-service and systems departments.

The root of the conflict between public-service and systems departments are the different orientations of the two specialties. *In general*, public-service staff approach their job from a tradition in which the needs of the library user are held in highest regard: providing universal access to information, treating every user's need for information with respect (regardless of how trivial or personally offensive that need may seem), and protecting user privacy are all core public-service values. From the public-service orientation, computers are simply tools for serving the public and computer knowledge is of value only insofar as it fosters access to information. Systems staff, on the other hand, *in general* approach their job from a computer-professional tradition in which protecting the integrity of computer resources, solving problems creatively, and deploying systems staff efficiently are core values. Systems staff tend to value computer knowledge for its own sake and have (or should have) more extensive knowledge of computer hardware and software than do public-service staff.

Given such different orientations, it is easy to see how conflicts arise. What a typical public-service person might see as an unnecessary delay in implementing some new hardware or software, a typical systems person might see as a prudent, absolutely necessary test period. What a typical systems person might see as a tidy technological solution to a given problem, a typical public-service person might see as a Big-Brother invasion of user privacy or a denial of access to information. Indeed, even the very language used by the two camps can be a source of conflict. While many systems people use the word *problem* to describe just about everything they deal with in the course of their work, some public-service staff are reluctant to stick the label of *prob-*

Organizational Structure and Culture

Whatever steps a manager takes to create a good working relationship between the public-service and systems departments, it is important that those steps be *in step* with the existing organizational structure. If the organization is hierarchical with a clear-cut chain of command, then any efforts to bring public service and systems together had best respect that hierarchy by involving all appropriate supervisors and moving within the proper channels. If the organization is team based, then you should operate in a team-based manner rather than trying to somehow impose your will on others via top-down directives.

Along with organizational structure, it is important, too, that you take into consideration the unofficial culture of your organization. Are there on-going feuds of which you need to be aware? Inter-departmental friendships that might be starting points for bringing whole departments together? Long-standing points of disagreement that are best avoided in the early stages of establishing good will? Is there a shared goal that both sides might be willing to work toward as partners? Developing a good awareness of unofficial corporate culture, especially when you are new to that culture, is essential for finding openings for improving cooperation as well as for avoiding pitfalls that can bring progress to a dead stop.

lem on anything involving library users. As divergent as the two orientations may be, both are necessary to provide public access to computers, and if the balance tips too far in favor of one orientation or the other, the results can be disastrous. Without systems staff protecting the integrity of computer systems, maintaining hardware and software, and planning for future improvements, there soon would be little in the way of computer resources for library users to access. On the other hand, without public-service staff advocating for the rights and needs of all users, the systems department can easily become the tail that wags the dog: a bureaucratic entity that grinds along for its own sake rather than working for those it is supposed to serve.

IMPROVING COMMUNICATION

There are a number of techniques a manager can use to increase co-operation between public-service and systems staff, and, as clichéd as it sounds, most of them involve improving communication.

INCREASE YOUR OWN COMPUTER KNOWLEDGE

As mentioned in Chapter 1, the more a public-access manager knows about hardware, software, and networking, the easier it is to communicate with systems staff. So learn as much as you can about computers. Join a computer-oriented listserv such as PACS-L or Web4Lib.[2] Keep an up-to-date computing dictionary at your desk and leaf through it from time to time, or regularly browse one of the many free online computing dictionaries.[3] Ask questions. The one thing you should not do, however, is try to fake it. If you don't know something, admit it and open yourself up to learn. After all, it is not your job to know everything there is to know about computers. That is why there are systems departments.

INTER-DEPARTMENTAL MEETINGS

Inter-departmental meetings, whether regularly scheduled or scheduled as needed, are one way to at least get a dialogue going if not to actually increase cooperation. If your organization is small, then informal one-on-one meetings may be appropriate; in a large organization, more formal group meetings may be needed to avoid the appearance of cliquishness. Whatever type of meetings you have, try to see that they are scheduled often enough to be useful but not so often that they become burdensome. If meetings occur but nothing seems to improve or get accomplished as a result, then some other approach is in order. After all, holding meetings is a means to an end, not an end in itself.

CROSS TRAINING AND ROTATIONS

If your organizational structure and culture permit it, consider cross training and/or rotations. In cross training, systems staff are trained to do public-service work, while public-service staff are trained to do systems work. Rotations put cross training to work by having staff from one department work in the other department a set number of hours each week. The value of cross training and rotations is that they lead to better understanding between departments and can foster cooperation.

If cross training and rotations are not possible (or are simply too radical for your organizational culture), look into the possibility of you and/or members of your staff sitting in as observers during systems-department training sessions. True, public-service staff might not get much out of such training, but showing an interest in how the other side operates may open doors of cooperation. Another possibility is to recruit systems-department staff to act as co-instructors for public-service staff-training sessions. This not only exposes systems staff to the public-service orientation, it sends the message that you value input from the systems department and are willing to cooperate.

WRITTEN COMMUNICATION

Written communication can be a good way to build relationships because it gives both sides a chance to think carefully about what they wish to say and also provides a record of what was said and agreed to. Paper memos are good for more formal communications, as when two sides are entering into an agreement of some import or a major request is made. E-mail is good for less formal communications and for keeping both sides up-to-date on rapidly changing situations. If you have an in-house public-service e-mail group to which you regularly send messages, consider asking one or more systems staffers if they would like to be included on the list. Similarly, you might ask to have yourself added to an in-house systems e-mail group. Remember, though, that the impersonality of e-mail, with its lack of visual and verbal cues, has led to many a misunderstanding.

SHARED GOALS

Identifying a goal shared by both the public-service and systems departments can lead to increased cooperation between the departments. The shared goal can be as simple as the chore of moving a few microcomputers from one room to another or as complex as configuring several dozen workstations to run under Windows NT. What is important is that it is a goal both departments share and which both departments can work together to achieve. Once you have identified a shared goal, you might offer the services of public-service staff in achieving it, perhaps volunteering to take on some low-tech part of the job while the systems department tackles the high-tech part. For example, the systems department might do the work of setting up a new piece of software and the public-service staff might do the in-house testing, reporting problems to the systems department as they occur.

When to Be an Advocate

No matter how cooperatively you work with your systems department, no matter how friendly your personal relationship with members of the systems staff may be, sooner or later there is going to be friction. As a manager of public-access computers, you must be an advocate for both your staff and for library users—two groups whose needs do not always mesh with the plans of the systems department. If you have done good work opening up the lines of communication and establishing solid working relationships, the inevitable points of friction will not burst into open flames. You may not always get everything your way, but by stating your case clearly, giving ground when you must, choosing your stands carefully, and keeping in mind that you are the systems department's direct *customer*, the interests for which you advocate will be well served.

SOFTWARE AND HARDWARE ACQUISITIONS

Typically, decisions about what software and hardware to acquire fall to the systems department. While this makes sense given the technological expertise of systems staff, public-service staff should nonetheless have some say in the acquisition process, and this say should come sooner rather than later. Ideally, an opportunity for input from the public-service department should be built in to all computer acquisition plans; if not, public-service managers must make their thoughts known—even if they feel that those thoughts are neither wanted nor welcome.

ESTABLISHING PRIORITIES

A principal duty of a systems-department manager is efficiently allocating the systems department's human and capital resources, including establishing priorities for which tasks will be completed and when. Before anything else, it should be a given that emergencies involving major public-access services—online catalogs, major databases, Internet connections—take first priority. Non-emergency priorities are not so clear cut, as public service is not the systems department's only customer: administration, technical services, circulation, and other entities are all competing for systems-department time and resources. The important thing is that public-service managers make sure public service is in the competition mix and that public-service priorities are not routinely shoved to the bottom of the systems department's to-do list.

POLICY ISSUES

Just because the systems department has the technology that can, in effect, establish and enforce computer-use policies does not mean that computer-use policy decisions should be left to the systems department. Any sort of computer policy that affects who can access electronic information resources or what resources can be accessed is much more a public-service issue than a systems issue. There must be input from the public-service side when it comes to user access.

PASSWORDS

Passwords are necessary to maintain the integrity of computer software, hardware, and networks, and they are typically controlled by the systems department. While public-service staff do not necessarily need every password used by the systems department, they do need those passwords that are necessary for them to do their jobs and should not be denied necessary passwords. For example, if a password is necessary to reboot networked public-access workstations, public-service staff should have that password. If not, then the systems department must be ready to respond *immediately* every time a workstation needs to be rebooted (including nights and weekends).

REPORTING COMPUTER PROBLEMS

Since public-service staff are usually the first to discover problems with public-access computers systems, it is they who end up reporting most problems to the systems department. Public-service staff need to report problems in an efficient, organized way so that the problems get fixed in the most timely manner and so that the systems department does not come to see public-service staff as a flock of "Chicken Littles." There are many things managers can do to improve the way computer problems are reported.

TRAIN YOUR STAFF

Everyone on your staff should be trained to recognize common computer problems and, as much as possible, should be trained to fix simple problems without calling on systems staff. For example, public-service staff should be able to recognize a simple paper jam in a printer and to fix it without help. Exactly what computer problems you train your public-service staff to handle depends on your situation. Your in-house systems department may prefer that virtually all problems, no matter how small, be fixed by systems staff only; in this case, your main training job will be teaching your staff to restrain themselves from fixing problems. On the other hand, your systems department may prefer that public-service staff try everything possible to solve a problem before calling for help. Whatever your particular situation, there are a few general things that public-service staff should know about computer problems:

- All public-service staff should be trained to recognize whether or not a problem is affecting a single workstation or the entire network.
- All public-service staff should be trained to report problems as completely as possible, providing enough details so that systems staff can best decide how to address the problem.
- All public-service staff should be trained to follow any formal procedures that have been established for reporting computer problems.
- All public-service staff should
  - ◆ know that simply rebooting a workstation fixes many computer problems.
  - ◆ know how to reboot a workstation.
  - ◆ always try rebooting a malfunctioning workstation before calling the systems department.

Tip Sheet

Identify Computer Hardware

For computer problems to be reported efficiently, individual computer workstations and printers must be readily identifiable. It is more efficient to report "Workstation 15 won't reboot" than to report "The workstation in the middle of the row by the windows won't reboot." Numbering workstations 1 through X is a good method of identification. As an alternative, if all your workstations are connected to the Internet you may choose to number each with the final digits of its IP address. If you have a large number of printers, identifying them by letters—"Printer K is out of toner"—can help to avoid confusing printers with numbered workstations.

WHO REPORTS COMPUTER PROBLEMS

Depending on the size and organizational culture of your institution, you may need to set up a formal procedure for determining who actually reports problems to the systems department. This can help to prevent the systems office from being swamped with multiple calls about a single problem. The reporting protocol may specify that all computer problems be reported to the senior public-service person on duty and that only he or she should report the problem to the systems department. Or your procedure may call for the first person who encounters a problem to make a note of it in the help-desk notebook and then report it to the systems department. If your operation involves multiple computer service desks, the reporting procedure may specify that when there is an apparent network-wide problem, the first service desk to discover the problem should call the other service desk(s) to see if others are experiencing the same problem and to determine who will report the problem to the systems department. Of course there are many ways to organize reporting procedures and many local considerations to factor in when developing procedures. The important thing is to come up with a logical, practical procedure that works well for everyone involved.

TO WHOM ARE COMPUTER PROBLEMS REPORTED

Even more important than who reports computer problems is determining who receives those reports. It is crucial that public-service managers get together with their systems counterparts to determine to whom problems will be reported. Probably the best solution from the public-service point of view is to have a single phone number to which all problems are reported. Whoever in the systems department picks up that phone is then responsible for logging the report and initiating action on it. One caveat is that this phone number should not dead end on a private office phone that is answered only when the occupant of that office is present; if it does, then there must be a backup number (or numbers) in case the problem is urgent and the primary number is not immediately answered.

If your systems department cannot accommodate a single-number solution like the one described above, then you and your systems department will need to create a chart that details who to call to report specific kinds of computer problems. For each type of problem, there should be a secondary number in case the problem is urgent and the primary number is not answered. A typical chart might look something like the following:

Ranganathan Public Library Reporting Computer Problems		
Problem	**Who to call**	**Number**
Individual PC	1. Jane 2. Paul	ext. 146 ext. 147
Printer	1. Luis 2. Doug	ext. 149 ext. 148
Network	1. Anne 2. Carol	555–1746 555–1785
Urgent night or weekend problem	1. On-call pager 2. On-call pager	555–3432 555–3524

Once you have created a chart for reporting problems it is important that your staff know where to find it and that you keep the information up-to-date. The public-service desk notebook is a good place to keep such charts.

Another way in which a manager can improve the reporting of computer problems is to use forms that are filled out by public-service staff whenever they report a problem. These report forms can be kept with the public-service desk notebook, or they can be used as the flip side of out-of-order signs that are taped to workstations while they are down. Once the problem has been solved, the form/out-of-order sign can be saved as record. Figure 7–1 shows a typical example of such a form.

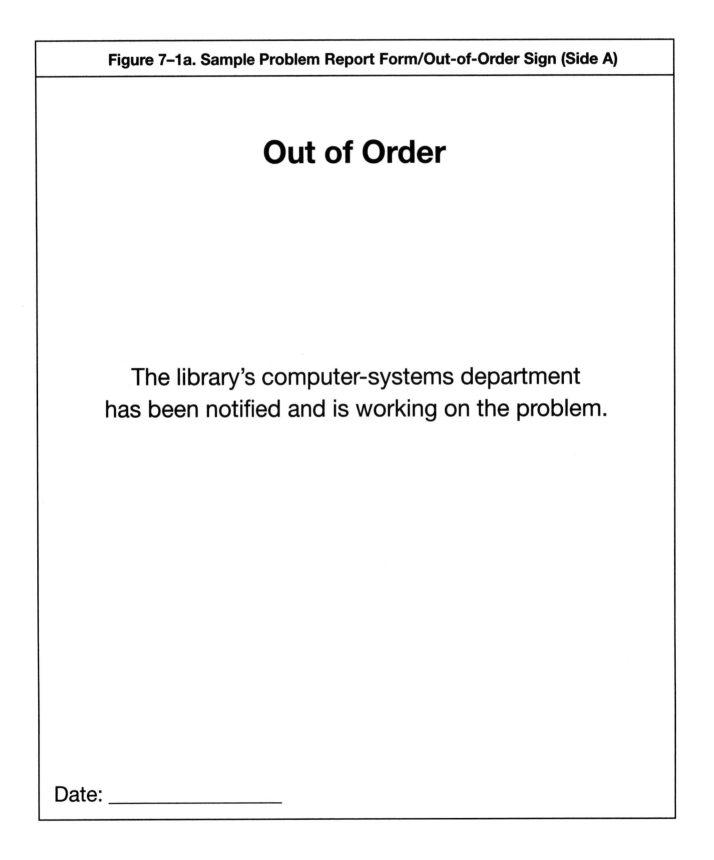

Figure 7–1a. Sample Problem Report Form/Out-of-Order Sign (Side A)

Out of Order

The library's computer-systems department
has been notified and is working on the problem.

Date: _____

Figure 7–1b. Sample Problem Report Form/Out-of-Order Sign (Side B)

Computer Problem Report

Date problem reported: _____ Workstation/Printer Number: _____

Reported by: _____ Reported to: _____

Type of Problem:

_____ Won't boot/boots to DOS prompt

_____ Blank screen

_____ 3.5" disk drive not working

_____ CD-ROM drive not working

_____ Won't access network

_____ Won't connect to Internet

_____ Freezes or crashes

_____ Won't print

_____ Other (Please describe in detail):

_____

_____

_____

_____

Date problem fixed: _____ Fixed by: _____

NOTES

1. By systems department, I mean those responsible for the more technical aspects of computing. Systems departments typically take responsibility for installing and maintaining of all computer hardware and software, for fixing hardware and software problems, and for installing and maintaining computer networks. Systems departments may or may not be in-house, and some of the above functions may be performed by in-house systems staff while others functions (in particular, networking) may be performed by the systems staff of a larger parent organization such as a university or library system.

2. To learn about what listservs are available, see the *Directory of Scholarly and Professional E-Conferences (n2h2.com/KOVACS)*.

3. For a list of online computer dictionaries see *Yahoo!*: Computing Dictionaries (*dir.yahoo.com/Computers_and_Internet/Information_ and_Documentation/Computing_Dictionaries*).

8 SECURITY

Imagine a library in which all the books are locked up in dark, climate-controlled rooms. Not only are these books never checked out, they are not so much as touched. No one could argue with the security of such a facility, though many would argue that you could not call such a place a *library*. In the real world, libraries must make trade offs between security and access, recognizing that any access at all compromises security. Just consider the recent case of the library user who, in the high-security environment of the Library of Congress reading room, repeatedly razor bladed valuable prints out of rare books. What is true for the security of print materials is also true for computers: access entails risk.

Security Truth Number One: There is no such thing as a completely secure *public-access* computer. If the public can access it, it is not perfectly secure; if it is perfectly secure, the public cannot access it.

Security Truth Number Two: Sooner or later every public-access computer operation, no matter how security conscious, is going to suffer some breach of security, be it hacking, computer viruses, vandalism, or theft.

Security Truth Number Three: There is such a thing as too much security. Public-access workstations can be locked down to the point where they are impossible to use in any productive way. Not only does overzealous security defeat the purpose of public-access workstations, it will never be 100 percent effective. Similarly, it is quite possible to spend far more money and effort on security than would ever be spent recovering from the worst depredations of hackers and vandals. The average library does not require Pentagon-style security for its computers, and no organization should spend $2,000 protecting a $1,000 computer.

SECURITY POLICY

Because perfect security is impossible, the best that managers can do is keep their public-access computers functioning day in–day out with as little security-related downtime as possible. When you put security goals in writing and then spell out standards and practices for achieving those goals, the result is a security policy.

The following statements, which are taken with permission (and a few slight modifications) from InFoPeople's extremely useful security

Web page (*www.infopeople.org/Security*) spell out security goals that could be adopted by almost any public-access computer operation:

- Computers should run day-to-day with little maintenance.
- Files on computers should be protected from changes. Temporary files and files downloaded or saved on the hard disk should be automatically removed.
- Only a pre-defined set of programs can be run. Public users should not be able to run programs downloaded from the Internet or brought in on floppy diskettes.
- Computers should be protected against virus infections and should not spread viruses to patrons' diskettes.
- System files such as the files in the Windows directory and the DOS root directory must be protected.
- The computer must be prevented from booting from a floppy disk. Booting from a floppy disk can allow full access to the hard disk and is a likely source of virus infections.

Whatever security goals an organization sets, the way it achieves them will vary according to the organization's computer resources, staff resources, user population, mission, and organizational culture. After all, even though public-access computers at both Silicon Technical University and Pleasant Creek Middle School need security, no one would expect both institutions to have identical security policies.

Even if the actual hands-on work of installing and maintaining security falls to the systems department, any security policy should be drafted with input from the public-service side of the house. It is important, especially, for public-service managers and staff to make sure that any security policy:

- Looks out for the interests of users as well as for the interests of the organization and its staff.
- Is practical and workable enough that it is likely to be enforced.
- Has been presented to, and openly commented upon by, everyone affected by the policy.
- Does not discriminate against any groups or individuals and does not violate any laws.

The remainder of this chapter presents only the rudiments of computer security. Computer security in its entirety is a topic that could fill a book by itself. One of the best books on computer security is Allen C. Benson's *Securing PCs and Data in Libraries and Schools*.[1] Though an updated second edition is badly needed, Benson's work is essential for anyone concerned about public-access computer security in schools and libraries. Another source for security information are the computer-security articles published from time to time in *Computer In Libraries* (some of these articles are also available online at *www.infotoday.com/cilmag/ciltop.htm*). Karen G. Schneider's article "Internet Librarian: Safe From Prying Eyes: Protecting Library Systems," (*www.ala.org/alonline/netlib/il199.html*) provides a good introduction to the entire topic of security for public-access computers.[2] InFoPeople's Public Access Computer Security for Windows 95/98 (*www.infopeople.org/Security*) contains a wealth of security information. Similarly useful is Monica King's *Workstation Security* (*www.leeric.lsu.edu/lla/1998_conference/workstation*), which provides a library-oriented overview of security issues and solutions. The Innovative Security Products (ISP) Website (*www.isecure.com*), though geared toward a corporate audience, provides useful information: both ISP's Security White Papers (*www.isecure.com/ispfyi.htm*) and Security FAQ (*www.isecure.com/faq.htm*) are worth a visit. Finally, LibraryLand: Electronic Resources: Public Access Software (*sunsite.berkeley.edu/LibraryLand/elres/soft.htm*) is an excellent source of information on security software.

PHYSICAL SECURITY

In the world of public-access computers, physical security is at least as important as system security. Such physical threats as theft, vandalism, and accidents all take their toll.

THEFT

Computers are tempting to thieves because they are valuable. Even if a thief cannot make off with an entire computer system, stolen computer parts such as chips and cards can be sold to computer "chop shops" or incorporated into the thief's own computer. Methods for preventing the theft of computers and their parts include:

INVENTORY

If you do not keep a complete and up-to-date inventory of what computer equipment you have, you might not even know if there is a theft problem. Having up-to-date lists of serial and property-tag numbers aids in recovering stolen equipment, and visible property tags deter thieves who would rather steal unmarked property. If your institution does not supply property tags, the *Thomas Register* (*www.thomas register.com*) lists some thirty vendors that sell property tags (look under the product heading Tags: Property). A sample inventory form is shown in Figure 8–1.

Figure 8–1. Sample Inventory Form			
Silicon Technical University Library **Public-Access Workstation Inventory Form**			
Workstation #			
Operating System	○ Mac	○ Win 3.X	○ Win 95	Win NT
Workstation Location			
Workstation IP Address			
CPU Brand			
CPU Model			
CPU Serial #			
CPU Property Tag #			
Monitor Brand			
Monitor Model			
Monitor Serial #			
Monitor Property Tag #			
Peripherals	○ External drive	○ Speakers	○ Scanner
Software Installed	**Software Version**		

LOCKS

Security cables and anchors, lid locks, CD-ROM drive locks, and computer furniture with locking compartments all deter theft. *Yahoo!*'s Computer Hardware Anti-Theft Web page (*dir.yahoo.com/ Business_and_Economy/Companies/Computers/Security/Hardware/ Anti_Theft*) lists the Websites of over twenty companies that manufacture anti-theft devices designed for use with computer hardware. Library association meetings and computer trade shows are good places to see computer locks and other anti-theft devices on display.

ALARMS

Motion alarms that sound off when anyone tries to move a computer are a deterrent in any situation, but they are especially useful for workstations located out of sight of a service desk. For public-access laptops, motion alarms are a must.

All emergency-exit doors adjacent to computer areas must have working alarms to prevent a thief from simply walking out with an armful of hardware. Any windows that can be opened should be alarmed or secured so they cannot be opened.

In libraries that use alarm-gate systems to detect uncharged materials, affixing detection tapes to computer hardware offers some measure of protection. Detection tapes are best placed inside hardware cases or in spots where the tapes are difficult to see. If you use detection tapes with computer hardware, experiment by carrying several pieces of hardware through the security gates to see how well the system works.

When any alarm sounds, staff should make a point of responding to it, even if they are sure that it is false. Thieves will soon learn not to fear alarms if they see staff routinely ignoring them.

CHECKOUT SYSTEMS

Having a checkout system for loose CD-ROM/DVD discs, headphones, microphones, and other walk-awayables may be labor intensive, but it is an effective way to curtail theft. Checking out keyboards and mice, though not the norm, reduces theft and can also act as a mechanism for rationing access to workstations.

WATCHFULNESS

Do not underestimate the power of an alert and watchful staff in deterring theft. The knowledge that staff might stroll though computer areas at any time will do as much as anything to keep potential thieves and vandals at bay. Good sight lines between workstations and service desks are a strong deterrent as well. In areas where sight lines are bad, concave overhead mirrors can improve visibility.

Tip Sheet

The Mouse Problem

Mouse pads, mouse balls, and the mouse itself are all favorite targets of thieves.

Short of the messy solution of gluing mouse pads to tabletops, the best way to deter the theft of mouse-pads is to set out the plainest possible pads. A drab gray mouse pad will sit undisturbed for months where one that features the school logo in flaming letters will disappear in a day.

Mouse balls are, for unknown reasons, regularly pilfered. One solution to this problem is to discourage theft by sticking adhesive plastic seals on the bottoms of mice or gluing shut the plastic collar that holds the mouse ball in place. Both of these solutions, however, make it difficult to open up the mouse for cleaning. Another solution is to abandon the traditional mouse for some type of alternative mouse such as trackballs or touchpad mice that are built in to keyboards.

Built-in mice also prevent theft of the entire mouse. If you would rather stick with traditional mice, cord locks that require a thief to cut the cord to get the mouse, thus rendering it useless, help reduce theft. Checking out mice to users is an extreme but effective anti-theft measure.

While asking staff to be watchful is fine, staff should not be expected to act as substitute security guards. For one thing, the role of security guard is not compatible with the role of helping the public; quite naturally, most users do not feel comfortable asking for help from a staff member who has just growled at them for some infraction of the rules. Nor should staff ever confront a thief, vandal, or other rule breaker if there is any chance of injury to the staff member or anyone else. If theft and rule breaking are truly out of hand, the library should hire professional uniformed security guards to handle such problems and let the public-service staff focus on its job of serving the public.

SECURITY CAMERAS

Though they smack of *1984*, security cameras are part of daily life for a reason: they deter crime. A traditional security camera system, though expensive, allows a single person to keep watch over many widely dispersed areas. A less expensive alternative to traditional security cameras, and one that is just beginning to come into its own, is the use of Web cameras for security. Web cameras can cost under $100 each, do not require the extensive wiring of traditional security cameras, can be monitored from any computer connected to the Web, and can be password protected to keep out unauthorized snoops.

An extremely low-budget alternative to security cameras are the fake security cameras sold in many retail electronics stores. These devices, which sell for around $30 each, look realistic enough to act as a deterrent—so long as their secret does not leak out.

VANDALISM

The same kind of watchfulness that deters theft also deters vandalism. It is especially important to think about vandalism when acquiring new computer furniture, as selecting vandalism-resistant surfaces and colors can save a lot of headaches down the road. Staff should be especially diligent about immediately reporting acts of vandalism, and all traces of vandalism must be erased as soon as they appear. Left untreated, any sign of vandalism—marking-pen graffiti, initials carved into a desktop, pried-off keyboard keys—becomes an open invitation for more of the same.

ACCIDENTS

Computers, while quite good at falling, are not very good at landing. Computer furniture that holds computer components securely in place will prevent unhappy landings—a feature that is especially important in earthquake country. Anything you can do to keep cords and cables from getting tangled up with feet will help prevent falls (of both computer components and computer users) and will cut down on damaged cables, bent cable connections, and loss of data due to the abrupt unplugging of a workstation.

Food and drink are not particularly healthy for computers, and for this reason no-food-or-drink policies have become standard in computer labs. Keyboards are especially vulnerable to dirt and dampness, so keyboard gloves—plastic keyboard covers which repel food, drink, and general grime—might be in order if spills are a significant problem. Power surges and outages are another kind of accident which can wipe out computers. Surge protectors and/or uninterruptible power supply units (discussed in Chapter 2, "Facilities") are a must.

If workstations sit beneath sprinkler systems, or if there are water pipes in the ceiling overhead, you should keep *immediately* at hand an adequate supply of plastic sheeting to throw over computer hardware in an emergency. Make sure all staff (including the evening circulation crew) know where the plastic sheeting is kept and why it is there. Once computer hardware has been soaked, insurance policies are a better option than repair shops.

If you are located in an area prone to floods or tropical storms, you should develop a plan for moving computer hardware to high ground in the face of impending inundation. Simply shifting hardware to an upper floor (preferably to an area without windows) is a viable option.

Any public building should, of course, have adequate fire extinguishers. Make sure staff know where fire extinguishers are located and are trained *by an expert* in how to use them (and when not to use them). Staff should be familiar with emergency telephone numbers, and notebooks with emergency information should be kept at every service desk.

SYSTEM SECURITY

When managers of public-access computers go looking for information on computer system security, they tend to get overwhelmed with information that is irrelevant to their needs. While issues such as network break ins, phone phreaking, encryption, and theft of confidential data may be important in the worlds of corporate and government computing, these are not major concerns at Middleville Public Library. Even much of the literature on computer hacking concerns types of hacking (such as attacks on Websites) that do not directly affect public-access computers. What managers of public-access computer should be concerned with is security for the microcomputer; in particular, with ways of preventing users from either intentionally or unintentionally damaging, disabling, or reconfiguring microcomputers. While the security of the local area network is also something of a concern in the public-access computer setting, LAN security is much more a matter for network administrators than for public-service staff.

There are two main approaches to microcomputer system security: One is to purchase off-the-shelf security software, while the other is to develop in-house security measures. There are pluses and minuses to each approach, and combinations of the two approaches are more the rule than the exception.

Focus On:

Physical Security And System Security

While most system-security solutions are software based, hardware also plays a role in system security. Computer-lid locks contribute to system security by preventing hackers from opening the computer case to remove or short out the CMOS battery—a common way to take control of a workstation. Similarly, drive locks prevent the use of a boot disk, which is yet another way for a hacker to take over a microcomputer. Drive locks also prevent the intentional or accidental introduction of disks that contain computer viruses.

A unique hardware-based device that contributes to system security is the Centurion Guard (*www.centuriontech.com*). Centurion Guard plugs into a microcomputer's disk drive and is then locked in place with a key. With Centurion Guard in place, all changes to the system are written to temporary files which are erased when the computer is rebooted. Even if someone hacks in and wreaks havoc, a simple reboot undoes all the damage.

OFF-THE-SHELF SECURITY SOFTWARE

Off-the-shelf security software provides, at least in theory, instant security. In actual practice, off-the-shelf systems always require tinkering. Indeed, no one would not want to acquire any security software that did not allow adjustment of the settings to meet specific local needs. Good security packages should also make it easy for system administrators to disable the security in order to make changes or perform maintenance on the microcomputer. The chief disadvantages of off-the-shelf security software are the costs, which can be prohibitive, and the fact that no security software, regardless of cost, is 100 percent effective. Also note that any security software must be thoroughly tested in-house to make sure it works well on the workstations and/or network on which it is installed, does not interfere with other software applications, and does not leave any security holes unplugged.

A list of security-software packages intended for use with microcomputers follows. The purpose of this list is not the endorsement of any of these products, but rather to give a sampling of what security products are on the market. Most of these software packages have, at minimum, the following capabilities:

- Prevent users from accidentally or intentionally accessing, viewing, renaming, or deleting crucial system files.
- Prevent users from downloading files to the hard drive and/or diskettes.
- Allow users to access approved software applications while denying access to forbidden applications.
- Allow administrators to set time limits on applications or workstation use.
- Track and record the use of applications, including Web browsers.

Additional features can include menuing capabilities, remote administration features (specifically the ability to logoff users from a remote location), Internet filtering, and the power to disable selected features of software applications. Anyone considering any security software package, whether listed below or not, should thoroughly research and test the product prior to purchase. The best way to get more information about any security package is to visit product Web pages, to seek out print and online software reviews, and to ask colleagues about their experiences with specific products. Security programs, and security in general, are frequently discussed on both the PACS-L (*info.lib.uh.edu/pacsl.html*) and Web4Lib (*sunsite.Berkeley.EDU/Web4Lib*) discussion groups.

CybraryN
Computers By Design
www.cybraryn.com

Desklock Security System
Starfield Software
www.starfieldsw.com

Everybody's Menu Builder
CARL Corporation
www.carl.org/pubaccess/mb1.html

FoolProof
SmartStuff Software
www.smartstuff.com

Fortres 101
Central Control
Cooler
Historian
Fortres Grand Corporation
www.fortres.com

Full Control
WinU
Bardon Data Systems
www.bardon.com

GS98 Access Control
DeskWatch
ArcSoftware
www.arcnet.force9.co.uk

IconHideIT
McLellan Software
www.mclellansoft.com/iconhideit

PCNanny
Net Nanny Software
www.netnanny.com/netnanny/pcnanny/pcnanny.htm

Program Selector Pro
Leithauser Research
members.aol.com/Leithauser/psp.html

Public Access Manager
Invortex Technologies
www.invortex.com

StopLight
StopLight NT
Safetynet
www.safe.net/products.asp

WINSelect KIOSK
WINSelect Policy
Hyper Technologies
www.winselect.com

Focus On:	
	Many Kinds of Hackers

RECREATIONAL HACKERS

Recreational hackers like learning about computers and enjoy the challenge of getting around the roadblocks thrown up by systems administrators. For the recreational hacker, hacking is a computer game *cum* learning experience, and a round of hacking ends with no harm done. Many recreational hackers contend that the term *hacker* should not even be applied to anyone who does harm to computer systems, but in general use *hacker* has come to include those who do harm as well as those who do not.

ETHICAL HACKERS

Ethical hackers are expert hackers who are paid (mostly by corporations) to hack into the payee's computer systems and report any security holes. While most libraries do not need to hire an ethical hacker, it is possible to assign trusted, computer-savvy library employees the job of trying to hack into library microcomputers to identify security holes. The subject of ethical hacking brings up an important point: some of the most serious hacking incidents are pulled off by insiders. A disgruntled or dishonest employee is, in fact, a much greater threat to computer security than the proverbial anonymous hacker sitting at a computer 2,000 miles away.

ACCIDENTAL HACKERS

Accidental hackers are users who, without intending to, do damage to computer systems. Accidental hackers may unknowingly delete system files or introduce computer viruses. Because most accidental hackers are not extremely knowledgeable about computers, simple security precautions will prevent them from doing any harm.

NUISANCE HACKERS

Nuisance hackers defeat security systems so they can do things that are not permitted on public-access workstations. The person who hacks into a public-access workstation to download a photograph of *Star Trek's* Seven of Nine and set it as Windows wallpaper is a nuisance hacker, as is the person who circumvents security software in order to play a computer game or check e-mail on a workstation where such activities are banned. While nuisance hackers may not cause any damage or break any laws, cleaning up after their handwork can be a nuisance.

DESTRUCTIVE HACKERS

Destructive hackers intentionally disable or destroy computer systems. Perhaps they do this because it gives them a sense of power, or perhaps they feel they are getting revenge for some wrong committed against them by the library, the school, the government, or whomever. Whatever their motivation, this is the type of hacker to fear the most.

CRIMINAL HACKERS

Criminal hackers violate the security of public-access workstations for the express purpose of committing such illegal acts as sending threats via anonymous e-mail, running confidence schemes, defrauding e-businesses, dealing in child pornography, and so on.

Understanding why hackers do what they do can be productive, but only insofar as it helps you come up with ways to thwart hacking behavior. When looking for ways to thwart hackers (and vandals), remember that anger is a lousy compass. Managers who are guided by anger—"I'll show those punks"—are likely to miss their mark. Of course it is infuriating when some smart aleck keeps resetting all the public-access Web browsers so that users go to a *South Park* fan page whenever they click the *Home* icon, but such behavior does not justify instituting a fascist security regime that makes life difficult for innocent users and staff alike. Also keep in mind that hackers are extremely unlikely to respond to reason, threats, warnings, policies, rules, and so on. To a great extent, hacking culture is about flaunting the rules, so putting up big, red-letter signs that read, "Do **NOT** download programs to the hard drives of these workstations" is more likely to increase instances of hacking than to reduce them.

A final, and often overlooked, point about hacking is that the persistence of some kinds of hacking can be a warning sign that the problem lies more with computer-use policies than with the hackers themselves. Say for example, that users repeatedly hack public-access computers to install a program that translates Windows commands into Chinese characters. No matter how many times staff remove the program, it keeps coming back. Perhaps the solution, in this case, is not tighter security but a better way to accommodate the needs of Chinese speakers? (A library history lesson: The Chinatown Branch of the San Francisco Public Library, which opened in 1921, did not begin to formally collect and integrate into its collection Chinese-language materials until 1970. Today, of course, the Chinatown Branch has an outstanding collection of Chinese-language materials, but the fact that a library, or any organization, could so conspicuously ignore the needs of its primary users for 50 years should be a caution to everyone who serves the public.)

For those interested in learning more about hackers and hacking, Wally Wang's *Steal This Computer Book*[3] is a somewhat irreverent beginner's guide to hacking techniques. Both *Phrack Magazine* (*www.phrack.com*) and *2600: The Hacker Quarterly* (*www.2600.com*) fall into the "Know Your Enemy" category of information sources. Though little of what is written in these publications has anything to do with public-access computers, both publications provide an informative inside look at hacker culture.

IN-HOUSE SECURITY

The alternative to purchasing off-the-shelf security is, of course, developing in-house security. The advantages of in-house security are that there are no up-front costs and that you can, given sufficient skill and knowledge, customize in-house security to do exactly what you want it to do and nothing more. The disadvantages of in-house security measures are that you genuinely need to know what you are doing and that you might spend so much time developing your security system that it would have been cheaper to buy an off-the-shelf security package in the first place. Before plunging into any in-house security project, it is a good idea to talk to colleagues who have experience in this area.

Windows policy editor

The widespread use of the Windows NT operating system and of stand-alone NT workstations has made the Windows NT Policy Editor (poledit) a popular way to develop in-house security. Setting policies with the Policy Editor allows you to fine tune what can be done, and who can do it, on any workstation, but using Policy Editor requires considerable knowledge of computers and is a job best done by a systems expert. Those who are interested in learning more about using Policy Editor can turn to the following sources: Ashley J. Meggitt and Tim Ritchey's book *Windows NT User Administration*,[4] Mike Nyerges' article "When the Internet Knocks, Unlock the Desktop,"[5] and the Web pages Setting Up a Public Access Computer Using Windows NT (*www.scpl.org/publicnt*) and Using Windows Poledit (*www.cadvision. com/redicks/security.htm*).

BACKUP SYSTEMS

The security provided by in-house and/or off-the-shelf security packages can be enhanced by the use of a backup system. Although the actual implementation may take considerable computer skill, the idea behind backups is fairly simple: First, start with a template workstation configured the way you want all your workstations to be configured. Then, make an archival copy (sometimes called a "disk image" or "clone") of the template workstation's hard drive and keep a copy (or, even better, several copies) in a secure place. If any workstation is hacked, reconfigured, or otherwise messed up, you can use the archival copy of the template to restore the workstation to its original state. Backup systems are also useful for configuring new workstations quickly and for insuring that every workstation looks and functions exactly the same. A good source for information on backup systems is InFoPeople's "Backup Considerations For Public-Access Computers" (*www.infopeople.org/Security/backup.html*).

Tip Sheet

CMOS Security Settings

Even if you use an off-the-shelf security package, in-house staff should enable each workstation's CMOS security settings. If the CMOS security settings are not enabled, a moderately skilled hacker can circumvent security software and, if so inclined, totally disable a computer.

CMOS is a battery-powered memory storage area in which such critical configuration data as the computer's boot sequence, date/time settings, drive types, and port speeds are stored. One way in which hackers take over computers is by shorting out or removing the CMOS battery, thereby resetting CMOS to its default settings and wiping out any CMOS security settings that may have been in place. As mentioned above, computer-lid locks prevent the shorting or removal of the CMOS battery.

A Word of Caution: Changing CMOS settings can totally disable a computer. Make sure you know what you are doing before making any CMOS changes.

CMOS PASSWORDS
On a computer on which no CMOS protection has been enabled, it is possible for anyone to access CMOS and change settings. Most often this is done by starting the computer and hitting a key or combination of keys before the operating system starts working. Creating a CMOS password prevents users from simply turning the computer off and on in order to access CMOS and change settings.

To create a CMOS password, start the computer and access CMOS. Many computers will tell you how to access CMOS by offering a prompt along the lines of:

Press <DEL> to access settings.

However, it may be necessary to consult the computer's manual to learn how to access CMOS. Once you have accessed CMOS, look for a menu item with a name like "password" or "security," and select it in order to create a password. Do not create a simple password that a hacker might easily guess—include both numbers and letters in the password and/or use a mixture of upper- and lower-case letters. Some computers will allow you to create two CMOS passwords, one of which allows you to reboot the computer and the other of which allows you to access CMOS and change settings. The former password can be given to public-service staff, while the latter is needed only by system administrators and so should not be widely distributed.

Continued

If you should set a CMOS password and then lose it, you may need to contact the computer's manufacturer for instructions on how to remove the password. On some computers this can be done by flipping a switch on the mother board or by pressing a particular key combination. In a pinch, you can wipe out a forgotten CMOS password by removing or shorting out the CMOS battery.

USING CMOS TO PREVENT BOOTING FROM A FLOPPY DISKETTE
Any user who can boot a computer from a floppy diskette can take over the computer or infect it with a virus. Drive locks and various types of security software can prevent booting from a floppy, but the best way to do this is to use CMOS to change the computer's boot-disk sequence. Normally, when a computer is turned on it looks for a boot program first in the A: (floppy) drive and then in the C: (hard) drive. Depending on the type of computer, you can change CMOS settings so that the computer either looks for a boot program in the C: drive before turning to the A: drive, or else never looks for a boot program in the A: drive. If you access CMOS and the method for changing the boot sequences is not obvious, look in the documentation that came with the computer or contact the manufacturer to learn exactly how to change the boot-disk sequence.

If you experience a disk crash after changing the boot-disk sequence, you will need to access the CMOS and re-do the settings so that you can boot the computer from the A: drive.

Backup software programs

There are a number of off-the-shelf software programs that can backup an entire hard drive and copy it to a storage device from which the copy can be rewritten to another workstation. Commercially available backup software programs include:

Altiris eXpress
RapiDeploy
Altiris
www.altiris.com

Backup Exec
Veritas
www.veritas.com/products/pi.html

Drive Image
Pro Powerquest
www.powerquest.com/usindex.html

HD98COPY
Gottfried Siehs
www.geocities.com/SiliconValley/Lakes/8753

Imagecast IC3
Imagecast
www.imagecast.com

Norton Ghost
Symantec
www.symantec.com/sabu/ghost/index.html

PC-Rdist
Pyzzo Software
www.pyzzo.com

Storage devices for backups

In order to store copies created by backup software, you will need a storage device of some type. If the backup files are small, a Zip or Jaz disk makes an adequate storage device, and some backup software is designed to span Zip or Jaz disks so that more than one disk can be used to store a copy of a single hard drive. Tape storage devices, on the other hand, have enough capacity that spanning is not necessary. If you have access to hardware for writing to CD-ROMs, you can employ it to make CD-ROM copies of the backup. What ever type of storage medium you use, it will be necessary to create a new archival copy every time there is a change to the template. When a workstation needs to be restored from an archival copy, the workstation must have some way of connecting to the storage device. For example, if you save the archival copy to a CD-ROM, each workstation you wish to restore must have either a built-in CD-ROM drive or the capability of being connected to an external CD-ROM drive.

Boot disk for backups

When you need to restore a hard drive from backup, you can often access the storage device through the microcomputer's operating system. If the microcomputer's operating system goes down, however, you will need a boot disk to access the storage device. The manual for your storage device should have instructions for creating a boot disk and loading it with the necessary drivers.

THIN-CLIENT WORKSTATIONS

Perhaps the ultimate public-access computer security solution, thin-client workstations eliminate the need to protect microcomputers by eliminating the microcomputer altogether. Something of a throwback to the days of the dumb-terminal OPAC, thin-client workstations have no hard drives for hackers to break into; instead, the processing is done on a server networked to the thin-client workstations. All that passes between the thin-client workstation and the server are keystrokes and screen paints. Thin-client workstations are much less expensive than microcomputers, but thin-clients require a robust server and an efficient network in order to work well. At present, thin-client technology is not widely used in the public-access setting, but it is a technology to watch over the next few years.

PASSWORDS

If you have security on your computers, then you most likely have computer passwords. In some cases, a single workstation (or group of workstations) may have multiple passwords: one for logging in regular users, another for users with special privileges, another for system administrators, and perhaps one or two CMOS passwords. In addition, bibliographic and full-text databases may require their own end-user and/or administrative passwords.

The most important thing about passwords is keeping the secret ones secret. A hacker who gets a workstation's CMOS password can thoroughly trash that workstation; a hacker who gets the administrative password for a library's network can do anything from shutting down the entire network to setting up a pirate Website on the library's server. One way to keep passwords secret is to not give passwords to those who do not need them. This includes users, obviously, but chances are that most staff do not need high-level administrative passwords; on the other hand, passwords should not be so closely held that front-line staff have to call in the systems department every time they need to login a public-access workstation. When you must distribute passwords to staff, never send them via e-mail, as there is a chance they will end up in the wrong hands.

On the opposite side of the coin, it is important not to lose passwords. If passwords are so numerous that they must be written down, be sure they are kept in a secure place. Little tricks like jotting passwords on the inside of your favorite manila folder or sticky-noting them to the bottom of your keyboard are not at all tricky to anyone rummaging for passwords. You could consider creating a Web page for storing lower-level passwords, but only if the Web page is mounted on a secure intranet or is password protected. Never put passwords on unprotected Web pages. Think twice about writing down high-level passwords in any form. Such passwords are best stored in human memory banks, though more than one person should know a key password in case the keeper of the password is incapacitated or otherwise unavailable.

When you create new passwords, keep in mind that hackers have password-cracking programs at their disposal. For this reason, a password made up of any common word or combination of common words is vulnerable. For example, a password like *treefrog* would be easy to crack. But because most passwords are case sensitive, a password such as *trEefRog* would be more difficult to crack. Even better would be a password along the lines of *trEe58%fRog*. Passwords based on any variation of your name, your institution's name, the name of the school mascot, etc., are asking to be cracked. Creating passwords by spelling words and names backwards does not make them harder to crack. Passwords should be changed periodically. If you notice a spate of security breaches, try changing passwords to see if that solves the problem. Another good time to change passwords is when an employee with knowledge of passwords leaves under unhappy circumstances.

COMPUTER VIRUSES

Computer viruses are software programs designed to spread themselves from computer to computer. Several hundred new computer viruses are discovered each month. Most of these viruses are virtually harmless joke viruses (for example the "Wobbling" virus which causes open computer windows to shake as if in an earthquake). A small percentage of computer viruses are capable of doing serious damage to microcomputers, servers, and the data they contain. There are two things you can do to fight computer viruses:

- Keep viruses off computers.
- Remove viruses from computers.

Keep viruses off computers

With few exceptions, computer viruses get on public-access computers in one of two ways: viruses are either downloaded over the Internet or introduced by infected diskettes. Computer security measures that prevent users from downloading files to workstation hard drives will prevent the downloading of viruses from the Internet (as well as prevent the clogging of the hard drive with downloaded software, images, sounds, and other assorted files). Drive locks will prevent users from introducing infected floppy diskettes to a workstation, but locking down disk drives leaves users with no way to save files for which they have a legitimate need. More user-friendly solutions include manually checking users' diskettes for viruses before they insert them, providing users with clean diskettes for saving files, and (best solution) installing antivirus programs that automatically check diskettes for viruses and remove viruses that manage to make their way onto hard drives.

Removing viruses from computers

The best way to remove viruses from computers is with antivirus software. Many companies produce commercial antivirus software, including:

F-Secure
www.datafellows.fi/products/anti-virus

McAfee
www.mcafee.com

Norton AntiVirus
www.symantec.com/nav

Trend Micro
www.anti-virus.com

Dr. Solomon
www.drsolomon.com/vircen

In addition, *Yahoo!* Virus Protection (*dir.yahoo.com/Computers_and_Internet/Software/Reviews/Titles/System_Utilities/Utilities/Virus_Protection*) provides links to the homepages of many more antivirus software manufacturers. Because new viruses appear constantly, it is important that whatever antivirus software you acquire is kept up-to-date. Licenses for antivirus software should include free updates, and the software itself should prompt you when it is time for an update. Good antivirus software should automatically scan for viruses but also allow a system administrator to run a virus check at any time.

Virus hoaxes

There are nearly as many virus hoaxes as there are actual viruses. When you hear about a new computer virus, there are a number of Websites you can visit to see if the virus is genuine or a hoax. These include

CERT
www.cert.org

Computer Virus Myths
kumite.com/myths

Internet Hoaxes
ciac.llnl.gov/ciac/CIACHoaxes.html

Symantec AntiVirus Research Center
www.symantec.com/avcenter

Never, never, never pass along news of a virus without confirming that it is a genuine. E-mailing warnings about a virus that turns out to be a hoax is an electronic *faux pas*, roughly equivalent to showing up for dinner at Buckingham Palace without a shirt.

Learning about viruses

Learning about viruses, and keeping informed about new viruses, is a good way to help keep them from becoming a problem. Intended for advanced computer users, Mark A. Ludwig's *The Giant Black Book of Computer Viruses*[6] thoroughly covers the topics of viruses and antivirus programs. The accompanying CD-ROM includes working examples of live computer viruses (be careful!). The antivirus software and virus hoax Websites listed above are all good sources of information on computer viruses.

Tip Sheet

Web Browser Security Issues

Web browsers can create security problems in a public-access computer setting by allowing users to:

- Send anonymous e-mail.

- Set any page on the Web as the browser's homepage.

- Set any image on the Web as Windows wallpaper.

- Make bookmarks to any page on the Web.

- Reset appearance preferences (for example, force all pages to display orange text on an orange background).

- Use the browser's **File**, **Open** features to delete or edit files on the hard drive.

There are a number of options for plugging the security holes created by Web browsers.

NETSCAPE NAVIGATOR 4 (STAND ALONE)[7]

This version of the popular Netscape browser offers all the Web browsing features of Netscape Communicator but does not include e-mail or newsgroups. Netscape Navigator 4 (Stand Alone) may be downloaded for free from the Netscape website (*www.netscape.com*).

Netscape can be made even more secure by renaming or removing the prefui32.dll file, as this prevents users from setting or changing Netscape preferences. Be aware, though, that sophisticated users can easily download a new copy of prefui32.dll and possibly reload it onto the hard drive.

INTERNET EXPLORER ADMINISTRATION KIT

The Internet Explorer Administration Kit (*www.microsoft.com/windows/ieak/en*) allows system administrators to customize the Internet Explorer Web browser by disabling any features that pose threats to security.

OPERA

The Opera Web browser (*www.opera.com*) is designed so that system administrators can easily disable user preferences. Two drawbacks of Opera are that 1) users are likely to be more familiar with Netscape or Internet Explorer than with Opera and 2) unlike Netscape and Internet Explorer, Opera is not freeware.

COMMERCIAL SOFTWARE FOR BROWSER SECURITY

A number of software companies sell software packages that allow system administrators to implement browser security by disabling certain browser features. The most popular software of this type is WINSelect KIOSK (*www.winselect.com*). Other software products that enhance browser security are listed on the LibraryLand Website (*sunsite.berkeley.edu/LibraryLand/elres/soft.htm*).

NOTES

1. Benson, Allen C. 1997. *Securing PCs and Data in Libraries and Schools*. New York: Neal-Schuman Publishers.
2. Schneider, Karen G. 1999. "Internet Librarian: Safe From Prying Eyes: Protecting Library Systems." *American Libraries*. 1 (January): 98–99.
3. Wang, Wally. 1998. *Steal This Computer Book*. San Francisco: No Starch Press.
4. Meggitt, Ashley J. and Tim Ritchey. 1997. *Windows NT User Administration*. Sebastopol, CA: O'Reilly.
5. Nyerges, Mike. 1999. "When the Internet Knocks, Unlock the Desktop." *Computers in Libraries*. 3 (March): 54–59.
6. Ludwig, Mark A. 1998. *The Giant Black Book of Computer Viruses*. 2nd ed. Show Low, Ariz.: American Eagle.
7. The following Websites offer detailed information on making Netscape Navigator more secure: Exploiting Netscape Navigator (*www.dayton.lib.oh.us/~kambitsch/netscape-hacks.html*); How to Lock-In IP Addresses on Netscape Navigator (*northville.lib.mi.us/tech/lockin.htm*); How to Edit Netscape for Public Access Computers (*www.infopeople.org/NS*); Netscape Unofficial FAQ (*www.ufaq.org*); and LibraryLand (*sunsite.berkeley.edu/LibraryLand/elres/soft.htm*).

9 STAFFING ISSUES

Public-access computers impact library staff in many ways. Crack reference librarians find themselves stumped over how to extract .zip files. Copy catalogers discover they have become experts at unjamming printers. Fuzzy cheeked student clerks know more about the inner workings of the library's computers than the senior administrators whose efforts brought the machines into the building in the first place. And the managers of public-access computers must work with any and all staff at their disposal to serve a public whose demand for help in using computers is as unbounded as their demand for access to computer resources.

WHAT DO PUBLIC-ACCESS COMPUTER STAFF DO?

The staff discussed in this chapter (and in the chapter on staff training and communication which follows) are those staff members who, as some part of their duties, directly help the users of public-access computers. This role distinguishes public-access computer staff from computer systems staff, whose chief function is the installation and maintenance of hardware and software. The help that public-access computer staff provide users is a public-service function similar to, and often intertwined with, traditional reference service and typically involves such duties as:

- Answering users' questions relating to computer hardware and software.
- Assisting users in using software applications.
- Solving computer problems encountered by users.
- Assisting users in searching for information on the Web.
- Assisting users in searching for information on the library catalog and proprietary databases.
- Providing assistance (chiefly via telephone) to remote users.
- Troubleshooting computer hardware/software problems and fixing those that do not require the expertise of systems staff.
- Enforcing computer-use policies.
- Supplying printers with paper and toner.
- Maintaining the overall security of computers and computer areas.

WHO STAFFS PUBLIC-ACCESS COMPUTERS?

Just who staffs public-access computers varies from library to library. A common thread, though, is that most libraries employ a mixed-bag of staff in this capacity. Public-access computer staff typically fall into one of the following categories:

LIBRARIANS

This category includes degree-holding librarians, most of whom come from the ranks of the reference department but who can, depending on the institution, also come from technical services, systems, special-collections, and even administration. Staffers of this type typically have a thorough understanding of libraries and a thorough commitment to the library profession. This commitment may or may not transfer to enthusiasm for assisting users of public-access computers. When librarians staff computer-service desks, it is not at all unusual for managers of public-access computers to find themselves supervising librarians who are either their superiors in the library organization or over whom they have no official managerial authority. Needless to say, such situations require considerable tact if they are to work successfully.

PARAPROFESSIONALS

This category includes full- or part-time library employees who do not hold library degrees but whose principal place of employment is the library. Paraprofessionals often bring to their work as much (or more) knowledge and professionalism as degreed librarians. Many paraprofessionals have years of practical library experience from which to draw, and it is not unusual to find paraprofessionals who are pursuing library degrees on a part-time basis. As with librarians, paraprofessionals who staff public-access computer labs can come from various departments in the library and possess varying degrees of computer knowledge. Like librarians, paraprofessional do not necessarily report to the public-access computer manager and may consider their duties in the computer lab secondary to their other duties.

STUDENT EMPLOYEES

Student employees[1] are typically part-time workers who do not necessarily see libraries as their chosen profession, though it is quite possible that they have considerable knowledge about computers, enjoy working in a library setting, and bring considerable enthusiasm to their work. Student employees almost never have the knowledge of libraries that librarians and paraprofessionals have, and their dedication to their job is mitigated by the demands of school. Student employees commonly report either directly or indirectly to the public-access computer manager, though this is not necessarily a given.

VOLUNTEERS

Typically found in public libraries, volunteer staff have the advantage of providing their services for free. On the downside, volunteers often require a large investment in training and supervision. Whether or not such an investment pays off is always a question mark, and the success of volunteer staff depends largely on the personality of the volunteer and the manager's mastery of the art of managing people who are not influenced by the all-important incentive of salary.

PART-TIME STAFF

Even if they are full-time library employees, all of the above employee types may be part-time public-access computer staff. Employees who work only part-time as public-access computer staff present the greatest challenge to the manager because—however good the intentions of such employees—their loyalties are divided. Consider this typical scenario:

> The library administration declares that John, a paraprofessional in the technical services department, will spend four hours per week staffing the public-access computer lab. Sally—John's supervisor and the person who writes John's annual performance review—is not thrilled that *her* valuable employee is spending four *fewer* hours per week doing the important work of technical services. For whatever reason, John usually shows up late for his shifts in the lab, always rushes out as soon as his shift over, and does not show much enthusiasm for his work in the computer lab. Even worse, John never comes to computer-lab staff-training sessions and so is never totally up to speed on lab policies and procedures.

As a manager, can you blame John? If you can, then you are making a bad situation worse. A more productive reaction would be to try to get John the training he needs to feel more comfortable and work more effectively in the computer lab. This may mean providing training in small doses: Short, one-on-one training sessions during John's shifts in the computer lab, easy-to-digest training tip sheets that John can read at the computer-lab service desk, or brief, not-too-frequent e-mails to keep John up-to-date on changes in the computer lab. More difficult to set right than training gaps are staff attitudes. Verbal or written pats on the back can do a lot to improve the attitude of someone in John's position—especially when you take the trouble to make sure his supervisor is made aware of the good work her employee is doing.

But what to do if none of your efforts pan out? What happens when, despite everything you try, the "free" help you are getting from another department is not working out? Speaking to the staffer's immediate supervisor is an option, but only if the immediate supervisor is not a root cause of the problem. In the end, if the amount of work actually done by a part-time staffer is not worth the time you put in (and grief you put up with) trying to work with him or her, it is time to politely decline the part-timer's services. This may sound obvious to the point of inanity, but there are many supervisors who continue to hang on to bad free help because they are so focused on numbers of staff hours that they fail to consider how much that free help is really costing them.

STAFFING LEVELS

Every manager of public-access computers would love to have an easy and indisputable answer to the question, "How much staff do you need?" While the one-word answer of *more* may leap into the mind of every manager who reads the above question, it is not an answer that is likely to move administrators who hear the word *more* about as often as they hear the word *hello*.

Instead of being simple and concrete, the answer to the question of how much staff is enough is complicated and abstract, hinges on many variables:

- How many public-access workstations do you serve and how heavily are they used?
- How staff friendly are your public-access workstations?
- How many different tasks are service-desk staff asked to perform?
- How much help does the staff provide and how extensive is that help?

HOW MANY PUBLIC-ACCESS WORKSTATIONS DO YOU SERVE AND HOW HEAVILY ARE THEY USED?

The most important determinants of the number of staff needed are the number of public-access workstations provided and the amount of use they get. The number of workstations is, of course, easy to calculate, but instead of expressing this number only as a simple integer—"We have 65 workstations"—it is more helpful to also express it as the following ratio:

$$\frac{\text{\# of workstations}}{\text{\# of public-access computer-staff hours per week}}$$

To show a very simple example, if your public-service-computer desk is open 90 hours per week, has 2 staff on duty at all times, and serves 65 workstations, your weekly workstation-to-staff-hours ratio would be 0.36. If the number of workstations increases to 80 but the number of staff hours remains constant, the ratio changes from 0.36 to 0.44. The advantage of using such a ratio is that if either the number of staff hours or the number of workstations change, the ratio reflects such changes in a way that is easily understandable. When faced with increased numbers of workstations and/or decreased staff hours, a chart showing how the ratio has changed over time provides convincing evidence that staff workload has, in fact, increased.

If you have a combined service desk (which will be discussed in greater detail later in this chapter) from which both computer assistance and reference help are dispensed, then figuring your workstation-to-staff-hours ratio is more complicated than if you have a computer-only service desk. In most cases, it will suffice to estimate what percentage of the staff hours on the combined service desk are devoted to computer assistance and use that figure in your ratio. For example, 270 staff hours are devoted to the service desk each week and you estimate that 70 percent of the assistance provided is computer-related, then the number of hours to use in your ratio is 189 hours per week.

How much public-access workstations are used is also quantifiable. There are three principal ways to track workstation usage:

- Tracking Software
- Sign-in/out Systems
- Observation

Tracking software

Using software to track workstation usage is a good option because software works around the clock, is unobtrusive, requires minimal staff time, and records information in electronic format for easy analysis. One disadvantage of tracking software is that, depending on user sign-in/out procedures, the software may undercount by not picking up the fact that User 1 has left and User 2 (or 3, 4, or 5) has taken over. Similarly, the software might overcount use if a user walks away and leaves an application running. For the above reasons, it may be worthwhile to consider implementing some type of sign-in/out system (see below) to supplement any tracking software.

If your public-access workstations are on a server, it is possible that your systems department can configure the server software to track workstation usage. If your workstations are already using security software (which is discussed in Chapter 8, "Security"), it is likely that the security software also has the capability of tracking usage and generating reports. Check the user documentation that comes with your security software or contact the software manufacturer to see if the software also tracks usage.

Sign-in/out Systems

Systems to keep track of how many users sign-in/out may be electronic or paper-and-pencil. Either way, a sign-in/out system should record user name, status (student, faculty, cardholder, visitor, etc.), and time/date in and out. You may require users to provide other information as well, but be aware that asking for too much information is intrusive and can inspire users to circumvent the system. Even asking for a user's name is somewhat intrusive, as names are not necessary if the purpose of sign-in is merely to track usage. Sign-in is much easier to control than sign-out, as there is not much you can do to prevent users from simply walking away from workstations when they are through. Collecting and holding IDs is one way to get compliance with sign-out procedures, though this can become a headache for both users and staff, especially on campuses where student IDs are also debit cards.

Electronic sign-in systems may be included as components of security or tracking software packages. It is also possible that your systems department can configure your server or workstations to require each user to sign in, although, once again, requiring users to sign out is a more difficult proposition. Some sign-in systems may require passwords. These can be permanent passwords (often based on library-card or student-ID numbers) or temporary passwords issued when the user checks in.

Paper-and-pencil sign-in/out systems can work well and have the virtue of simplicity. Sign-in sheets with blanks for users to fill in can be kept in a ring notebook or on a clipboard. Sign-in sheets are best placed on a service desk that users must pass by as they head for the public-access workstations. Disadvantages of paper-and-pencil sign-in systems are that users may fail to sign in, staff may have to spend time reminding users to sign in, and the information collected on paper must be manually converted to electronic format for easy analysis. This latter problem can be avoided if the paper sign-in sheet is replaced with a computer into which users type their sign-in information. For example, you can use a database program such as Access or FoxPro to create an electronic form that each user fills in at the service desk before using a workstation. Whether it employs paper-and-pencil or database software, any sign-in system that resides at a central service desk is next to useless if users do not have to pass by that service desk on their way to the public-access workstations. And as mentioned above, requiring users to sign out is more difficult than requiring them to sign in.

Observation

A third, and quite valuable, tool for measuring workstation usage is to make observations of how much, and possibly how, workstations are being used. The observation process itself consists of no more than staff members walking around the public-access workstations at designated times, recording what they observe on pre-printed forms.

The set of rules that spell out exactly how you will make observations, how you will record the information obtained from the observations, and when and how frequently you will make observations is determined by your research design. To create a scientifically valid research design, you will want to either consult books on research design or consult with someone who is an expert in this area, such as a statistician. A scientifically valid research design is good in any case, but it is vital if you wish to publish the results of your observations or present them in some formal way.

What follows is a simple research design for observing workstation usage. While it is not perfect (no research design is), it will serve for any usage study intended for internal use.

Sample research design

The design of the form on which observations are recorded is crucial for a successful research design. All forms should include spaces for the date and time that the observation was made and for the name of the observer (in case you need to check back with the observer to resolve questions). In the simplest case, you may choose to record only whether or not a workstation is in use at the time the observation is made. A sample form for recording this type of observation is given in Figure 9–1.

Figure 9–1. Sample Form For Simple In-use/Not-in-use Observations

Computer Use Observation Form
Ranganathan Library Computer Lab

Date of Observation: _____

Time: _____

Observer: _____

Workstation	In Use	Not
1		
2		
3		
4		
5		
6		
7		
8		
9		

Instead of simply recording whether a workstation is in use or not in use, you may choose to record exactly what each workstation is being used for at the time of the observation. The specificity of the categories listed on the form will depend on exactly what kind of information you wish to record. For example, the form might have the category of "Internet" for any use of the Internet, or it might subdivide Internet into categories such as "Internet Research," "Internet Games," "Internet Chat," and so on. If you choose to make observations of exactly what each workstation is being used for, you may run into issues of user privacy. In particular, you will find that some users do not like library staff peeking over their shoulders while taking notes on a clipboard. None of this necessarily rules out making detailed observations, but it is good to be aware of such potential problems before you begin observing. A sample form for making detailed observations is given in Figure 9–2.

Once you have created a form, you and members of your staff should test drive it to see how practical it is in real-life use. You may find that you need to change categories. Or that the check boxes are not big enough. Or that the form works better if printed in landscape instead of portrait format. Whatever problems you find, correcting them ahead of time is better than dealing with them in the midst of a study. The piloting period is also a good time to train staff in how to make observations. Chances are observations will be made at times you are not present (nights and weekends), so it will be necessary to train various staff members on how to make and record observations.

With the form in good working order, the next question is when and how often to make observations. One option is to pick a single week and make observations on two weekdays and one weekend day during that week. (This is assuming your public-access workstations are available seven day per week.) You can use the roll of a die to randomly pick two weekdays (1 = Monday, 2 = Tuesday, 3 = Wednesday, 4 = Thursday, 5 = Friday, and 6 = roll again) and one weekend day (odd = Saturday, even = Sunday). Divide each randomly chosen day into 15-minute increments and print up enough forms so that you and your staff can make observations every 15 minutes on those days. If making an observation every 15 minutes is too much to handle, you can divide days into half hours or even into hours. Be aware that making fewer measurements each day increases the chances for a skewed result. Also note that making observations exactly on the hour or half hour may skew results if those times have a major impact on the routines of your users. Class-change times that fall on the hour are one such example. The week you choose to make your observations can also skew the results. In a school or college setting, choosing the week of July 4th will produce a much different result than choosing a week in the middle of October. To avoid such skewing, try to

Figure 9–2. Sample Form For Making Detailed Usage Observations

Computer Use Observation Form
Ranganathan Library Computer Lab

Date of Observation: _____

Time: _____

Observer: _____

Workstation Number	Library Catalog	Internet	E-mail/ Chat	Data-base	Word Processor	Not In Use	Other
1							
2							
3							
4							
5							
6							
7							
8							
9							

select a week that reflects typical usage. Of course there is no reason that you cannot make observations during more than one week. You might make observations for three weeks in a row. Or you might make observations over a long period of time, perhaps randomly choosing one week out of every month (or one week out of every two months) for making and recording observations. The more data you collect, and the longer the period of time over which you collect it, the more accurate picture you can draw. The caveat here is that making observations is so time consuming that collecting data can impact staff resources. Try telling your library administrators, "I need more staff because the staff I have is busy collecting data to prove that I need more staff," and see how far it gets you.

Once you have made observations and recorded the data from them, you will want to put your data in some type of electronic format—most likely an electronic spreadsheet such as Lotus or Excel. Once that is done, you can draw some conclusions from the data even without statistical expertise: On average, what percentage of the workstations are in use at any one time? What applications (Netscape, library catalog, word processor) are used most often? What times of day and/or days of the week get the heaviest use? For more detailed analysis of your data, you may want to consult with a statistician, though be prepared for your consultant to send you back to the drawing board if you did not discuss your research design with him or her before launching your study.

HOW STAFF FRIENDLY ARE YOUR PUBLIC-ACCESS WORKSTATIONS?

There is a lot said about the user friendliness of computers, but not much attention is paid to staff friendliness. Staff-friendly computers are important to managers because they require fewer staff than do staff-unfriendly computers.

The most important factor of staff friendliness is the extent to which workstations and peripherals are self service. Everything that users can do for themselves—sign in and start using a workstation, select the software application they want from a clearly presented menu of choices, choose a CD-ROM disc from a self-service rack or cabinet—frees up staff to help with more complex matters. By the same token, every unautomated function that staff are required to carry out means an extra burden. If, for example, it is library policy that users will not use Web chat in the computer lab, it is much better to come up with an automated technical solution that prevents users from chatting rather than handing staff the burden of shooing users off Web chat sites. Not only are such duties time consuming for staff, they are also stressful. As a manager, you should always be on the lookout for ways

Focus On:

Cholera And Uncommon Sense

In September 1854, London was suffering from a cholera outbreak that would kill 500 people before it was through. Dr. John Snow (1813–1858), a pioneer in the field of public health, looked at a map showing where cholera cases had occurred and observed that the outbreak was centered around a single water well. Snow correctly concluded that this well was the source of the disease.

What does this have to do with public-access computers? The point is that data itself is worth nothing if we cannot draw accurate conclusions from it. Many intelligent people had the same data Snow did, but only Snow was able to draw the right conclusion from the data. Almost as important is the fact that Snow was able to draw the right conclusion even though at the time nobody, including Snow, had all the information on the problem—namely, that cholera is caused by bacteria.

Once Snow came to his conclusion about the water well, there were any number of things he and the civil authorities might have done. They could have put up a sign warning people not to drink the water. They could have stationed watchmen at the well to warn people away. Moved everyone out of the neighborhood and burned down the buildings. Or done nothing at all. What Snow did, however, is legendary in its brilliance—he ordered the well's pump handle removed. Once this was done, the cholera outbreak subsided almost at once.

The point to this second part of the story is that not only is it necessary to draw good conclusions from data, it is also necessary to take good actions based on those conclusions. If the act of collecting and analyzing data does not either 1) cause you to change the way you do things or 2) confirm that a course of action you are already taking is the right one, then all the work of collecting the data was wasted.

to turn services that require assistance into self-service or automated functions.

Security and reliability also play a role in staff friendliness. Unsecure computers eat up hours of staff time spent removing viruses, reinstalling software, cleaning out downloaded files, and (in bad cases) reformatting hacked hard drives. Similarly, unreliable computers that constantly freeze up or otherwise malfunction demand a lot of staff time and expose staff to the stress of dealing with unhappy users.

Finally, the layout of public-access workstations is an important component of staff friendliness. If workstations are laid out so that staff can get to them easily and can see what is going on from a central service desk, relatively few staff can serve a large number of workstations.

The ideal situation would be to have public-access workstations that are both user friendly and staff friendly, but sometimes there is a trade off between one kind of friendliness and the other. Workstations that are locked down tight to prevent hacking are friendly to staff, but if they are locked down to the point where users cannot access files on floppy diskettes, then they are no longer friendly to users. In such cases, managers may have to make judgment calls about which kind of friendliness—user or staff—is more important.

HOW MANY DIFFERENT TASKS ARE SERVICE-DESK STAFF ASKED TO PERFORM?

The number of tasks that service-desk staff perform affects the amount of staff needed. Any service desk at which staff provide help exclusively with computer-related questions can get by with less staff than one at which staff are asked to perform a variety of additional tasks such as answering reference questions (face-to-face or on the telephone), answering directional questions, checking out library materials, acting as *de facto* security guards, and so on.

HOW MUCH HELP DOES THE STAFF PROVIDE AND HOW EXTENSIVE IS THAT HELP?

The first part of this question points to a staffing factor that is reasonably easy to quantify: How many times each day does the staff help users? A paper-and-pencil form kept on a clipboard at the service desk is still the best way to keep track of staff-user interactions. As anyone who has worked at a service desk knows, however, just because such a form is the best way to track transactions does not make it the perfect way. Staff inevitably forget to mark down every user transaction—especially when things are busy. Forms get lost, and there are errors in transferring the collected data from the paper form to an electronic database. This latter problem can be eliminated by replacing paper-and-pencil forms with computerized data-collection forms, but requir-

Focus On:

Combined-Service Desks

A combined-service desk from which both computer and reference help are dispensed is a common scenario in libraries. For the library, the advantage of a combined-service desk is that it allows fewer library staff to serve more users; for library users, the advantage is that they do not have to decide whether their question is a reference question or a computer question and so do not end up getting shuttled from one service desk to another. Indeed, users' questions are often hybrid questions that are not neatly classifiable as either reference or computer questions.

The disadvantage of a combined-service desk is that library staff who are good at providing reference service are not necessarily good at providing computer assistance, and vice versa. One solution to this problem is to provide training to bring staff who are weak in one area up to speed. Another solution is to provide some kind of back-up system so that staff who are hit with a question (be it computer or reference) they cannot handle can call on the services of a staff member who can. The back-up system might involve pairing up staff members who have complementary skills to work the same shifts at the service desk, or it might mean designating mentors—computer and reference—who can be called on when help is needed in their area of expertise.

It is possible to have staff at a combined-service desk wear badges that identify their particular strengths—"Computer Assistant" or "Reference Librarian"—but users are unlikely to pay much attention to such badges when they need help. Also, fostering strict specialization among the staff could potentially produce a situation where a computer assistant refuses to direct a patron to a dictionary or a reference librarian declines to show someone how to open up a Web browser.

Even when computer- and reference-service desks are separate, cross training and good communication are essential, as library users will inevitably ask reference questions at the computer desk and computer questions at the reference desk.

ing staff to enter each transaction into a computer is likely to result in even less compliance than there is with paper-and-pencil forms.

At library reference desks it is standard practice for staff to categorize the questions they answer by type—often under the headings of *directional* or *reference*. It is also standard for no two librarians to agree on what precisely constitutes a reference question and what constitutes a directional question. For a computer-service desk, it is more practical to categorize user transactions by the amount of time each takes to handle rather than by some abstract measure of difficulty. Figure 9–3 provides an example form:

Figure 9–3. Computer Help Desk Statistics Sample Form			
	< 1 Min.	1–5 Mins.	5–10 Mins.	> 10 Mins.
8:00–10:00				
10:00–Noon				
Noon-2:00				
2:00–4:00				
4:00–6:00				
6:00–8:00				
8:00–10:00				

Using the Figure 9–3 form can give you data on how much time staff actually spends assisting computer users. This is good information to have, but it does not really answer a more significant question: Does the staff, on a transaction-by-transaction basis, spend too much or too little time helping users? Ideally, staff will spend enough time on each transaction so that the user does not feel frustrated or abandoned, but not so much time that staff are unable to help every user who needs assistance. Is this balance being achieved? How do staff members decide that they have spent enough time with one user and need to move on to help other users? Is it up to each individual to decide? Has the staff come to an unwritten water-cooler consensus on helping users? Or is there a written policy for providing help to public-access computer users.

Though not necessary in all situations, a written policy for providing help to users can aid staff in developing a confident sense of how much help is enough. In addition, such policies can be turned to for support when users complain about a lack of help or favoritism in providing help. Before attempting to write out any such policy, however, it is important to consider if it is necessary or wise. If interactions with users run smoothly and show all signs of continuing on that course, there is little point in drafting a written policy. If, however, staff is being run ragged providing in-depth help, or if users are regularly unhappy with the level of help they receive, then a written policy may improve the situation. Before starting work on any policy, it is important to get staff input; failing to involve staff in the process of writing a policy will all but insure that it will be ignored. Another important consideration when writing a policy for providing help is taking into account the library's overall mission. Does the mission emphasize a *teaching* role in which it is essential that users learn as they are being helped, or does the mission lean towards a *results-oriented* approach in which a successful end result matters more than how it is achieved? Or does the mission point towards some middle ground approach? Does the library's mission statement recognize different categories of users (faculty versus students versus non-students; cardholders versus non-cardholdes; adults versus juveniles) and call for different levels of service for different types of users?

If you choose to pursue a written policy, remember that there are far too many hardware configurations, software programs, functions, and commands to spell out exactly what staff will and will not provide help with in every situation. Policies, in most cases, will tend to be comprised of general standards rather than specific dictates. For example, a policy standard might put general time limits on providing help:

Sample Standard 1: Computer-lab staff will help any one user for no more than five consecutive minutes when others are waiting for help. After five minutes, the staff member will politely break off to help others and will return to provide more help only after others have been assisted.

Another type of standard might suggest a way for busy staff to avoid becoming tangled up in an especially complex or arcane problem:

Sample Standard 2: If the computer-lab staff on duty have done all they can to assist a user—including consulting help screens and printed documentation and calling on any available back-up staff—and are still unable to come up with a satisfactory solution or answer, they will give the user the option of scheduling an appointment to meet at a later date and time with a member of the staff who will have had the opportunity to investigate the problem in more detail.

While general standards are the rule, concrete standards might be necessary to speak to specific problem situations that arise regularly:

Sample Standard 3: While e-mail and chat are not forbidden in the computer lab, staff will not assist users in using e-mail or chat applications, including Web-based applications such as *Yahoo!* Mail, HotMail, and so on. The reasons for this are 1) e-mail and chat are not central to the library's mission, and 2) there are too many such programs for staff to become familiar with all of them.

Of course the above examples are simply that—examples. Any help standards you adopt should be shaped by local experience and circumstances. And by common sense. Although the above examples all place limits on the extent of help provided, it is important to remember that a policy can give as well as take away. It is quite possible that you and your staff could develop a policy that calls for staff to provide more extensive help with applications that are core to the library's mission. For example, a music library might provide especially extensive help with *Music Index*, or a medical library might go the extra mile to provide help with a CD-ROM application that prepares medical students for their medical licensing examinations. And any library at all might choose to provide extensive help with its own online catalog.

Akin to policies for providing help is the issue of the consistency of the help provided from one staff member to the next. Say, for example, that the Excel spreadsheet is one of the software applications offered on your workstations. The rule (written or unwritten) is that staff will help users with basic Excel commands but will not provide help with the advanced statistics functions that are part of the program. One person on the staff, however, is working on a graduate degree in statistics and sees no reason not to help users with the statistics functions in Excel. While the users she helps are pleased with the service, the rest of the staff is starting to tire of hearing comments like, "Why can't you help me set up a covariant analysis? That one woman who works here helped me do it last week."

One response to such a dilemma is to let everyone on the staff provide whatever level of help they are willing and able to provide. After all, one might argue, staff with special skills should not be hamstrung just so everyone else can keep pace with them. An opposite response is to forbid staff from providing more than a specified maximum level of help on the grounds that doing so is not fair to the rest of the staff and, in an educational setting, may be tantamount to doing students' assignments for them. A middle response is to allow staff who wish to provide help that goes above and beyond the norm to do so, but only if they first make it clear to the user that they are getting a level of assistance that they can't expect all the time. Of course stating such a caution is no guarantee that users will hear or heed it. It is also important to emphasize to staff who wish to go above and beyond the norm that they must provide such help to everyone who needs it, not just to a select few.

SCHEDULING STAFF

When it comes to the number of staff hours at their disposal, the situation for front-line managers is more often summed up as, "Take it or leave it," rather than, "Tell us what you need and we will provide it." However many staff hours are provided, at minimum a manager must have enough staff hours to schedule at least one staff member on each service desk during every hour that the public-access workstations are available to users. Additionally, there must be enough staff redundancy to cover vacations, sick days, and other circumstances that pull staff away from their service-desk duties. Beyond the minimum staff levels, it is desirable to have enough staff hours to put extra staff on service desks during busy times.

It is possible, though not feasible in all settings, to stretch staff hours by making public-access workstations available to users at times when no staff are on duty at the computer-service desk. If this is done, it should be during slow times, such as early mornings and late evenings, and it is crucial that unstaffed workstations be especially secure from hackers and vandals. Any plan for leaving workstations unstaffed must enlist the cooperation of other library public-service staff, as users with computer questions will inevitably make their way from unstaffed workstations to reference desks, circulation desks, and other points where staff are present.

Another staff-stretching alternative is to provide users with a conspicuous help phone that they can use when no staff are present. The best help phones are those that are pre-set to automatically dial a specific number as soon as they are picked up and which cannot be used to dial any other number. Any help phone that can be used to dial other numbers will soon be transformed from a help phone into a free public phone. A similar solution is to use an inexpensive push-button pager system (available from most electronics retailers) that allows users to summon help by pushing a button on a transmitter box. The transmitter box can be placed at a service desk or in some other conspicuous location. Explanatory signage can be helpful with both the help phone and pager arrangements. It is important to remember that phone or pager systems can only stretch staff hours so far: there still must always be a staff member at the other end to receive and respond to the calls and pages.

Depending on the number of persons involved in staffing your public-access workstations, you may find it helpful to keep a portion of your staff on a regular schedule. For example, Jack from cataloging might prefer to work the computer-lab desk from 8:00 to 9:00 A.M. every Monday and Wednesday, week in and week out. Work-study students Sylvia and Ali always take the Tuesday and Wednesday night shifts. And so on. Along with those staff on a regular schedule, it is good to have some floaters who can fill in to cover miscellaneous times as needed.

If possible, you should print out and distribute the weekly service-desk schedule at least a week in advance. This allows time for adjustments as staff discover that they have conflicts. Again, depending on the number of staff involved, you may wish to develop a formal procedure for staff who need to make changes after the schedule has been distributed. This might include setting a minimum lead time (2 days, 24 hours, etc.) for requesting changes to the schedule. Or you might develop a form for requesting schedule changes. In most libraries, public-service staff routinely make last-minute swaps with each other, and in such cases the person originally scheduled for a time slot has the responsibility for coordinating the swap and making sure his or her replacement will be there. Another wrinkle to scheduling is that the schedule for public-access computer staff will need to be coordinated with the reference schedule if there is a combined-service desk for computer and reference help.

Scheduling can be a time-consuming and sometimes frustrating chore, but do not discount its importance. There is something of an art to maintaining a schedule that is tight enough to keep chaos at bay yet flexible enough so that staff (especially part-time staff from other library departments) feel their needs are being accommodated. Figure 9–4 presents a sample weekly staffing form. Figure 9–5 presents a sample request form for schedule changes.

Figure 9–4. Sample Weekly Staffing Schedule Form

	Monday	Tuesday	Wednesday	Thursday	Friday	Saturday	Sunday
8:00	1. ___	1. ___	1. ___	1. ___	1. ___	Closed	Closed
9:00	1. ___	1. ___	1. ___	1. ___	1. ___	Closed	Closed
10:00	1. ___ 2. ___	1. ___ 2. ___	1. ___ 2. ___	1. ___ 2. ___	1. ___ 2. ___	1. ___	Closed
11:00	1. ___ 2. ___	1. ___ 2. ___	1. ___ 2. ___	1. ___ 2. ___	1. ___ 2. ___	1. ___	Closed
12:00	1. ___	1. ___	1. ___	1. ___	1. ___	1. ___	1. ___
1:00	1. ___ 2. ___	1. ___ 2. ___	1. ___ 2. ___	1. ___ 2. ___	1. ___ 2. ___	1. ___	1. ___
2:00	1. ___ 2. ___	1. ___ 2. ___	1. ___ 2. ___	1. ___ 2. ___	1. ___ 2. ___	1. ___	1. ___
3:00	1. ___ 2. ___	1. ___ 2. ___	1. ___ 2. ___	1. ___ 2. ___	1. ___ 2. ___	1. ___	1. ___

Figure 9–4. Sample Weekly Staffing Schedule Form *Continued*

	Monday	Tuesday	Wednesday	Thursday	Friday	Saturday	Sunday
4:00	1. _____ 2. _____	1. _____ 2. _____	1. _____ 2. _____	1. _____ 2. _____	1. _____ 2. _____		
5:00	1. _____	1. _____	1. _____	1. _____	1. _____	1. _____	1. _____
6:00	1. _____ 2. _____	1. _____ 2. _____	1. _____ 2. _____	1. _____ 2. _____	1. _____ 2. _____	1. _____	Closed
7:00	1. _____ 2. _____	1. _____ 2. _____	1. _____ 2. _____	1. _____ 2. _____	Closed	Closed	Closed
8:00	1. _____ 2. _____	1. _____ 2. _____	1. _____ 2. _____	1. _____ 2. _____	Closed	Closed	Closed
9:00	1. _____	1. _____	1. _____	1. _____	Closed	Closed	Closed

Figure 9–5. Sample Request For Schedule Change Form

Request for Schedule Change

Your Name: _____

Date and time you would like to change: _____

Date this form submitted: _____

Submitted to: _____

Forms must be submitted at least 24 hours in advance of change. For changes made less than 24 hours in advance, you are responsible for finding someone on the staff to cover for you.

Request approved: _____

Not approved: _____

NOTE

1. I exclude from this category student employees who are also library-school students. Such employees have more in common with paraprofessionals and librarians than with the typical student employee.

10 COMMUNICATING WITH STAFF AND STAFF TRAINING

COMMUNICATING WITH STAFF

To state the obvious, the two principal ways to communicate with staff are through speech and writing. Speech has the advantage of being the most interactive form of communication, assuming everyone involved is willing to listen and respond (not always a given). Speech is also the best medium for attaching emotional nuances (approval, concern, anger, etc.) to a message. As common and important as speech is, there are some problems with it as a form of communication: Speech has a greater potential for being misunderstood than does written communications and speech rarely leaves you with a lasting record of exactly what was said. Unless you hold a meeting (see below), speech is not an effective way to communicate with a large number of people. You can, however, use mass voicemail to send a spoken message to a large number of people at one time. The best use of mass voicemail is to send a brief reminder to a large number of people—"Don't forget tomorrow's staff-training session. It's at 2:00 in the upstairs classroom."—or to send information you would rather not write down, such as a new computer password. Voicemail, though, is not a good means of two-way communication, as anyone who has played voicemail tag can attest, and it is useless for communicating with those on your staff, such as student workers, who are not on the office voicemail system.

WRITTEN COMMUNICATION

Though not as interactive as speech, written communication has several advantages. Composing written communications requires senders to think about and organize what they wish to communicate. Good writing also leaves less room for misinterpretation by the receivers of the message; creates a lasting record of exactly what was communicated; and is an efficient way to communicate with a large number of people. Written communication tends to be perceived as more formal than speech, which may or may not be an advantage depending on the message you are trying to send.

Paper communication

Written communications on paper still has its place. In fact, in the world of non-stop e-mail, a paper document has more impact than ever. If some major change is in the offing—perhaps there is going to be an expansion to the computer lab or some major policy change is on the way—writing it up as a formal memo and distributing it to all concerned is a good way to give the announcement appropriate weight. Especially-important memos can be printed on letterhead stationery for even greater impact.

Another good way to keep staff informed via print is a brief monthly (or bimonthly) newsletter covering the public-access computer operations. Staff newsletters are easily created with desktop-publishing software such as Microsoft Publisher or Adobe Pagemaker, and they can be run off on a copy machine rather than printed. Distributing occasional "tip sheets" (as shown in Figure 10–1) is a good option if producing a newsletter is impractical. It is good practice to print newsletters and tip sheets in standard formats, as this gives them a distinctive appearance when they turn up in a pile of office mail and also provides a sense of continuity from one installment to the next. Consistently publishing staff newsletters or tip sheets on a single color of paper is another way to give them a familiar and distinctive look. It is a good practice to archive newsletters or tip sheets at the service desk and encourage staff to read them when things are slow.

Finally, an old-fashioned service-desk notebook (spiral is best) is still hard to beat as a means of written communication. Everyone on the staff can make entries in the notebook to keep track of problems, suggest solutions, blow off steam, and otherwise communicate. The main drawbacks of a notebook are that it is easily lost and that staff may need to be regularly reminded to read it.

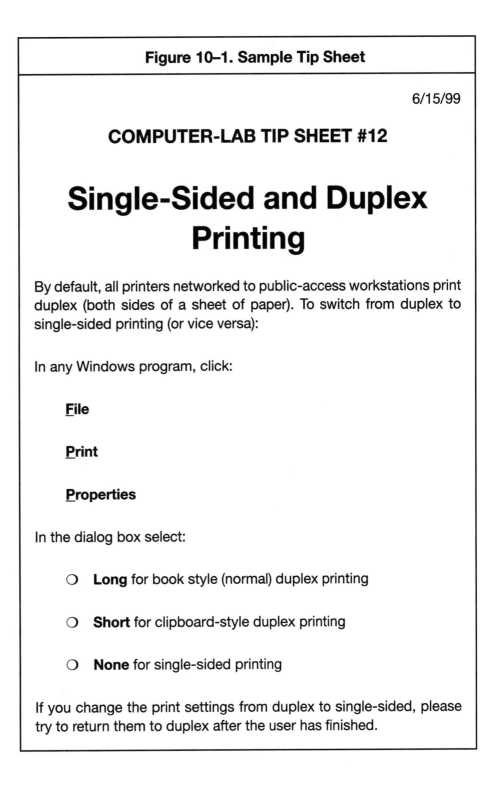

Figure 10–1. Sample Tip Sheet

6/15/99

COMPUTER-LAB TIP SHEET #12

Single-Sided and Duplex Printing

By default, all printers networked to public-access workstations print duplex (both sides of a sheet of paper). To switch from duplex to single-sided printing (or vice versa):

In any Windows program, click:

File

Print

Properties

In the dialog box select:

○ **Long** for book style (normal) duplex printing

○ **Short** for clipboard-style duplex printing

○ **None** for single-sided printing

If you change the print settings from duplex to single-sided, please try to return them to duplex after the user has finished.

E-mail

E-mail can be an effective way to communicate with staff, either individually or *en masse*. By creating a staff e-mail group, a manager can instantly send a single message to a large number of people at one time. When using e-mail to communicate important information, be careful to avoid the tendency to dash off a quick "hey bob waddabout lunch?" type of e-mail. If you do send e-mail messages of this type, staff will not take them seriously. Think of e-mails to your staff as formal communications and take the time to make sure they are correct in both form and content. Not only will this cut down on confusion caused by carelessly worded e-mails, it will indicate that you have sent an important message, not something that you pecked out with one finger while talking on the telephone. You may want to give your group e-mails a running title ("Labogram," "Computer Flash," "Lab News," etc.) in the subject field so that when staff receive a group e-mail from you they will know that it contains important information about public-access computers. Figure 10–2 presents a sample e-mail for staff announcements.

Figure 10–2. Sample E-mail Message

To: labstaff

Subject: Lab News: New Printer Will Be Installed on Tuesday

cc: wstevens

Lab News: New Printer Will Be Installed on Tuesday

Just wanted to let everyone know that Systems will install the new Computer Lab printer at 9:00 A.M. this Tuesday. It should take about two hours. Users will not be able to print while the new printer is being installed. We have already put up signs in the lab announcing this.

The new printer is able to print on both sides of a sheet of paper (duplex printing). Users will be able to choose whether they print one-sided or duplex, but the default will be to print duplex. If you do not know how to switch back and forth from one-sided to duplex printing, there is a new Tip Sheet on the staff Web page that tells how to do it. I've also printed out this Tip Sheet and put it in the service-desk notebook. See me or Jenny if you have any questions.

Susan

A few additional heads-up on e-mail:

- E-mail does not work at all for staff who do not have (or refuse to use) e-mail; it does not work well for staff who do not regularly check their e-mail.
- Keeping e-mails short and sending as few as possible will give each e-mail you send greater impact. Flooding staff with a nonstop stream of e-mail chatter is as bad as not communicating at all. Do not become an e-mail blabber mouth.
- E-mail, though conversational in feel, lacks the visual and verbal clues of speech. Concepts like humor and irony do not travel well via e-mail and very often provoke hurt feelings or outright anger.
- E-mail is not secure. Do not use e-mail to transmit information such as computer passwords, comments about individuals, or anything else that you would not want printed on the front page of the local newspaper.
- Once sent, an e-mail cannot be taken back. Before sending an e-mail to staff, take a minute to make sure that you have said what you intended to say, that the information is correct, that there is nothing in the message you may regret later, and that you have not written anything in all capital letters (WHICH READS LIKE SHOUTING).

Yet another e-mail option is to establish a listserv for your staff. Rather than being primarily a one-way communication from the manager to the staff, a listserv allows everyone on the list to contribute to the discussion. Such a dialog may result in better ideas and better service, but there are potential problems:

- Listservs have been known to break out in angry flame wars.
- The job of moderating a listserv can become time consuming.
- Staff who belong to the list may unsubscribe if the number of messages becomes too high, the climate on the list becomes unfriendly, or the list routinely drifts off topic.

WEB COMMUNICATIONS

If you or someone on your staff is handy at creating Web pages, the Web can be a good means of communication. Web versions of newsletters and/or tip sheets are one possibility, as is a Web-based staff manual. Web-based information has the advantage of being accessible from many locations and is easy to update. Because Web-based information does not land in staff in-boxes the way print and e-mail documents do, you will need to provide reminders pointing staff to new or changed Web documents you would like them to peruse. Of course

Tip Sheet

Staff Manual for Public-access Computers

Creating a staff manual that outlines policies and procedures for public-access computers is a good way to provide necessary information to your staff. Such a manual might include:

- Computer-lab hours

- Opening and closing procedures

- Policies

- Passwords (only if manual is kept secure)

- List of databases and/or software available

- Instructions for using key databases and/or software

- List of hardware available

- Instructions for using hardware (printers, scanners, etc.)

- Troubleshooting protocols

- Numbers to call when computers, printers, or networks go down

- How to handle emergencies (fire, bomb threats, disturbances, etc.)

- How to handle non-emergency situations (hacking, user complaints, etc.)

Exactly what goes into the manual will depend on your local situation. The information in the manual might be divided up by topic or perhaps presented in a Frequently-Asked-Questions (FAQ) format. However the information is presented, there should be an index or table of contents so staff can quickly find what they need.

Printed copies of the manual are handy for staff who are trying to assist users, so keep a current copy at the service desk. Because the manual will be updated frequently, be sure that all printed copies are dated and/or given a version number and that old versions are disposed of or archived when a new version appears. Announce new versions of the manual to staff and suggest that staff read it to bring themselves up-to-date on changes.

Mounting a staff manual on the Web is also a good idea. Staff can access the Web version of a manual whenever they wish, and it is easy to update. If you use the Web version of the manual as your master copy, you and your staff can print out copies of the Web version whenever hard copies are needed.

putting information on the Web doesn't do much good if staff do not have convenient access to the Web, and you must never post staff-only information (such as passwords) on unprotected Web pages. If your organization has a secure intranet, it is safe to post confidential staff-only information on it. It is also possible to password protect Internet Web pages, though this is usually not as secure as using Web pages that are on an intranet.

With bulletin-board software,[1] it is possible to create a Web bulletin board for public-access computer staff. Similar to an e-mail listserv, a Web bulletin board allows everyone to participate in the conversation by either posting a new message or commenting on an existing one. Old messages are automatically archived for later retrieval. Unless a Web bulletin board is on a secure intranet or password protected, you and your staff must not post confidential information to it. Unlike listserv messages, messages posted to a bulletin board do not turn up in e-mail in-boxes—staff will need to visit the bulletin board to access any messages posted on it.

MEETINGS

Meetings can be an extremely expensive way to communicate. If you tie up ten staff members in a meeting for an hour, their combined salaries for that hour are likely to add up to more than the cost of an hour of satellite broadcast time. Few managers would order up an hour of satellite time willy-nilly, but many will call a meeting for next to no reason. Not only are meetings costly, there are often so many that staff come to loathe meetings in general. While it is inevitable that you will call meetings to discuss important matters with your staff, there are some things you can do to make your meetings successful.

- Make sure any meetings you call are about something important. If you find yourself racking your brain for items to fill up your agenda, chances are the meeting is not necessary.
- Do not schedule meetings more frequently than they are needed. One busy and productive monthly meeting is better than two half-speed biweekly meetings.
- Do not schedule meetings to run any longer than necessary. Meetings are almost always scheduled to last at least an hour, but there is no reason you cannot schedule a 15- or 30-minute meeting if that is enough time to take care of the business at hand.
- Solicit agenda items well in advance of the meeting. A few days prior to the meeting, put the agenda in writing and distribute it to those who will attend. Within reason, stick to the agenda during the meeting. Be sure to start and end meetings at the times

printed on the agenda. Once you develop a reputation for starting meetings right on the dot and for putting the most important items at the top of the agenda, stragglers will learn to come
on time.

- Make sure meetings are interactive, not one-way monologues.
  The only reason to go to the expense and trouble of a meeting is
  to provide a venue for back-and-forth communication. When
  one-way communication is all that is required, it is better to distribute the information in written form. If you are chairing a
  meeting, do not let any one person (yourself included) dominate.

- Do not waste valuable meeting time going over items that can
  be better taken care of in other venues. For example, you might
  meet to actively discuss staff policy changes, but you would not
  waste meeting time simply reading through policies—staff can
  do that on their own.

Focus On:

Change And Communication

One of the most difficult things about working with computers is dealing with change: new software, new versions of once-familiar software, new databases, new developments on the Web, new procedures and policies instituted on the local level. All this change can be overwhelming to staff. Good managers can help staff deal with the weight of change by communicating well about change.

In order to reduce the stress caused by constant change, managers need to stay on top of technological changes, decide (to the best of their ability) which changes will really impact staff, and communicate the news of truly important changes in a way everyone on the staff can understand. For example, when free Web e-mail services such as HotMail and *Yahoo!* Mail started coming on strong in the late 1990s, it proved to be important news for people working in public-access computer settings. Suddenly users of public-access computers were sending and receiving e-mail over the Web in an entirely new way, asking for help with e-mail services staff had never heard of, and sidestepping prohibitions against sending and receiving e-mail in computer labs where the practice was banned. By picking up early on this e-mail development, making staff aware that it would have an impact on them, and planning how staff should respond to the change, a manager could have saved staff the stress of suddenly discovering that the world of e-mail had changed in a significant way.

On the other hand, a manager can also reduce change-related stress by helping staff not worry about changes that will not have much impact on their duties. If an agitated staff member says something like, "I just heard about this terrible software that lets anyone at all add text to any Web page they want. It's going to turn the Web into a graffiti jungle," it is up to the manager to find out about the software and supply staff with the facts—which are always less dire than the hype.

Beside sweeping technological changes that impact the entire world, your staff must also deal with local changes that affect policies and

Continued

procedures: a new database is now available to users, there is a new password for the public-access workstations, the library administration has decided to end free printing for users, and so on. Some local changes, such as a new password, must be communicated quickly and must be communicated to *everyone* who has a need to know. One of the worst things a manager can do is to leave some staff out of the loop when important new information is being communicated. Being left out is frustrating and makes staff feel that they are not valued. Less-urgent local changes can be saved up and communicated all at once, perhaps via a weekly or monthly announcement. Whether the staff prefers to hear about changes one at a time or would rather digest several changes at once is something for the manager to get a feel for. What is most important is that the manager communicate changes clearly and consistently.

Timely training can also help ease the stress of change. Even a major change, such as switching from a Windows 3.x operating system to Windows 95/98, is less stressful when staff feel well prepared to face the change. Ideally, such training should be provided far enough ahead of the change so that staff will be prepared to face the change, but not so far ahead that the training has been forgotten by the time the change actually hits.

Finally, managers can help staff deal with change by communicating, over and over, two simple ideas:

1. In the world of computer technology, change is the normal state of affairs, so it is wise to develop a mindset that expects change rather than one which is surprised or upset by it.

2. No one, no matter how knowledgeable, can keep up with all the changes in technology, so don't feel bad if you cannot stay on top of everything.

STAFF TRAINING

Staff training goes hand-in-hand with communication because much of what a manager communicates to staff is, in one way or another, training. Training is an important issue for managers because effective training is necessary for good public service. For staff, training can building confidence and morale, but it can be a source of discontent if staff feel they receive either too much or too little training, if the training they receive is ineffective, or if some staff members are left out of the training loop.

TRAINING FOR ALL

Too often, training is provided hit or miss. Maybe there was a staff training session on the new scanner when it was installed (a year ago), but anybody who could not attend that training session or who has joined the staff in the last 12 months has been left to their own resources. Maybe someone else on the staff gave them a quick run through. Maybe they played around with the scanner on their own, more or less figuring out how it works. Maybe they have never learned to use it at all and hope that no users ask them for help with it. When training is provided (or not provided) in this way, it creates a situation which can divide staff into knowledge haves and have nots. This is a bad situation for users who need assistance and a bad situation for those staff who are unlucky enough to end up in the "have not" camp. Or maybe being unlucky has nothing to do with it; sadly, age and gender biases sometimes play a part in determining who gets training and who does not.

The worse-case scenario for knowledge haves and have nots is the "Doug Syndrome." This occurs when library users are told something like, "Oh, you'll have to come back when Doug is working. He's the only one who knows how to help you with that." Whether the Doug Syndrome is due to Doug's desire to monopolize his special knowledge or due to the rest of the staff's unwillingness to learn, good managers actively stamp out the Doug Syndrome by making sure that knowledge is spread among the staff.

One thing that managers can do to make sure everyone on the staff is a knowledge "have" instead of a "have not" is to develop a staff-training checklist that spells out the *essential* things that all staff should know. The key to creating such a list is to include everything that is truly essential while leaving off everything that is not. As much as you might like to have a truly comprehensive checklist, any such list would be overwhelmingly long (a too-long list can be broken up into "Basic" and "Advanced" lists that staff can tackle one at a time). Input from staff is crucial in creating a staff-training checklist, as no single

Tip Sheet

Universal Skills and Local Lore

Some of the training your staff requires will touch on universal skills. These include techniques or procedures that do not vary from one location to the next; for example, how to open applications in Windows 95, how to locate and use Web search engines, how to copy files to diskette using a Mac computer. It is quite possible that newly hired staff will come to the job already possessing all or most of the universal skills they will need to do their jobs. If not, managers have the option of turning to ready-made training materials (either in print or on the Web) that can teach staff the universal skills they need.

Training staff in matters of local lore is another thing altogether. Even the best and brightest new staff are not going to come on the job already knowing where the printer paper is stored—much less where to find the key that opens the storeroom door. New staff will not know who to call when the network goes down on the weekend or the password that lets them logon as administrator so they can delete the pornographic wall paper a user has left on one of the workstations. This type of local knowledge has to be taught by the manager or the manager's proxies, and not even *amazon.com* can sell you a book called *Everything You Need to Know to Work in the [fill in the blank] Library Computer Lab (For Dummies)*.

Because local lore can become second nature for experienced staff (including managers), it is easy to forget to pass all of it along to new staff. That is why including local lore on a staff-training checklist is a valuable tool for making sure new staff (and under-trained staff) are given all the information they need to perform their jobs well.

person can hope to know everything that should and should not go on the checklist.

Once the staff-training checklist has been developed, it can be issued to each current staff member and to new staff as they come on the job. Whether or not completing the checklist is a formal requirement for staff, such a checklist makes it easy for trainers to make sure they have covered all the essentials and for staff to identify gaps in their knowledge. Of course, any such checklist is a living document to which new items must be added and from which old items must be weeded. Keeping a staff-training checklist up-to-date requires effort, as does keeping staff informed of changes to the checklist. Figure 10–3 is a sampling of items (both local lore and universal skills) that could go on a staff-training checklist. What would go on your checklist would depend entirely on your local situation and on what you and your staff consider essential skills and knowledge.

SELF-STUDY TRAINING MATERIALS

As even the most boiled-down-to-the-essentials staff-training checklist suggests, you and your staff could spend a lot of time providing and receiving training. Managers, therefore, need to make training as efficient as possible. One way to do this is to provide staff with self-study training materials. Self-study materials can reduce the amount of time trainers have to spend with trainees and can make time spent together more productive by eliminating or reducing the need to hash over the basics. Trainees can use self-study materials at their own pace and at the times that best suit them; the latter is especially beneficial for part-time staff who work nights and weekends and so cannot easily attend weekday training sessions. Another benefit is that self-study training materials can be perused during slow times at the service desk. Of course self-study materials cannot entirely take the place of human-to-human training, and they are not the best solution for all training needs. It is up to you as a manager to decide whether self-study or trainer-based training is the most efficient way to meet a particular training need.

Self-study training materials can be as informal as a simple list of instructions for carrying out a routine procedure, such as opening and closing a computer lab, or as complex as a multi-page tutorial that teaches all the ins and outs of searching the online catalog or using Windows 95. The trick to developing effective self-study training materials is to keep the materials as simple and straightforward as possible and to be willing to change them based on feedback you receive from staff. What follows are examples of some of the forms that self-study training materials may take.

List of instructions

A list is a logical format for a routine procedure. The key to creating a good list is to keep it as short as possible. Be sure to test lists with several guinea pigs to make sure nothing is left out and that the instructions are clear. Lists like the following can be kept in service-desk notebooks or mounted on staff Web pages for quick reference.

Figure 10–3. Sample Self-Training Checklist

COMPUTER LAB

Staff-Training Checklist

FAMILIARITY WITH TRAINING MATERIALS
- ❑ Read computer lab manual
- ❑ Locate print/Web versions of lab newsletter, tip sheets, etc.
- ❑ Included on lab-staff e-mail list.

OPENING AND CLOSING ROUTINES
- ❑ Read "Lab Opening and Closing Procedures"
- ❑ Knows passwords for logging on workstations
- ❑ Opened lab at least one time (with supervision)
- ❑ Closed lab at least one time (with supervision)

EMERGENCY PROCEDURES
- ❑ Who to call for life-threatening (actual or potential) emergencies
- ❑ Procedure for evacuating building
- ❑ Locations of fire alarms and fire extinguishers
- ❑ Fire extinguisher training (conducted by building-services staff)
- ❑ Phone tree for major computer emergencies (network down, etc.)

LAB PRINTER
- ❑ Restock paper
- ❑ Unjam printers
- ❑ Reroute print jobs to circulation-area printer
- ❑ Cancel print jobs
- ❑ Pay-to-print system (copy cards, etc.)
- ❑ Change toner cartridge
- ❑ Switch between one-sided and duplex printing
- ❑ Printing Web pages that have white text on dark backgrounds
- ❑ Phone tree for printer problems

VIRUSES
- ❑ Run virus check on hard drives and disks
- ❑ Reporting procedure for viruses found on lab workstations
- ❑ Virus confirmation Web pages:
    CERT *www.cert.org*
    CIAC *ciac.llnl.gov/ciac*

HARDWARE BASICS

- ❑ Turn on/shut down computers, monitors, printers, scanners, etc.
- ❑ Knows passwords for logging on workstations
- ❑ Connect and disconnect cables and plugs
- ❑ Troubleshoot cables and plugs
- ❑ Lock and unlock computer security cables
- ❑ Troubleshoot drives (CD-ROM, Zip, floppy)
- ❑ Remove 3.5" diskettes accidentally stuck in Zip drives
- ❑ Phone tree for serious hardware problems

Scanner

- ❑ Turn scanner off/on
- ❑ Scan image using Corel software
- ❑ Resize, rotate, and crop images using Corel
- ❑ Save images as files
- ❑ Scan text using Omnipro software
- ❑ Save scanned text as a file

WINDOWS 95 BASICS

- ❑ Read "Windows 95 Introduction" (in lab manual or on staff Web page)
- ❑ **Start** button to run applications (Netscape, WordPerfect, etc.)
- ❑ Windows 95 **Help** features
- ❑ **Shortcuts** (add, remove, copy)
- ❑ **Taskbar** (add items to and remove items from)
- ❑ Add and remove icons from **Desktop**
- ❑ Switch between open applications
- ❑ Minimize all open applications
- ❑ Open a new document
- ❑ Open an existing document
- ❑ Name or rename a file or folder
- ❑ Save to or access A: drive
- ❑ Save to or access Zip drive
- ❑ Access CD-ROM drive

Task Manager

- ❑ Reboot

Windows Settings

- ❑ Shut down or restart computer
- ❑ Access settings

Figure 10.3 *Continued*

Figure 10–3. *Continued*

❑   Set display area
❑   Set colors
❑   Set wallpaper
❑   Set screen saver
❑   Set font size

Windows Explorer
❑   Log in as administrator (Explorer not available under user login)
❑   View the contents of drives and folders
❑   Create folders and files
❑   Move folders and files
❑   Delete folders and files
❑   Copy folders and files
❑   Rename folders and files
❑   Recover deleted files
❑   Format a diskette

FILE FORMATS
❑   Convert files from one format to another
❑   Open ASCII text files using word processor or other application

Identify the following common file formats

❑ .doc	❑ .wpd	❑ .xls	❑ .ppt	❑ .txt	❑ .pdf
❑ .htm	❑ .html	❑ .jpg	❑ .bmp	❑ .gif	❑ .tif
❑ .mpg	❑ .avi	❑ .wav	❑ .hqx	❑ .zip	❑ .tar

BASIC NETSCAPE
❑   Back
❑   Forward
❑   Go
❑   Reload
❑   Stop
❑   Open location
❑   Open local file
❑   Print
❑   Save
❑   Bookmark
❑   Launch software/databases with Netscape
❑   Set browser preferences

ADVANCED NETSCAPE
- ❑ Download helper applications
- ❑ Adobe Acrobat Reader software
- ❑ Telnet within Netscape
- ❑ RealPlayer software

Locate & use Web search engines and directories
- ❑ Basic *Altavista* search
- ❑ Advanced *Altavista* search
- ❑ *Yahoo!*
- ❑ *Excite*
- ❑ *Metacrawler*

DATABASES
- ❑ Access databases from lab workstations
- ❑ Access databases remotely
- ❑ Assist users who report problems with remote access
- ❑ Password for databases that require passwords
- ❑ Choose appropriate database(s)
- ❑ When to refer questions to reference librarians

Database concepts & functions
- ❑ Records
- ❑ Fields
- ❑ Keyword (free text) search
- ❑ Subject (fixed vocabulary) search
- ❑ Boolean logic
- ❑ Limit searches to specific fields (Author, Title, Date, Subject, etc.)
- ❑ Citations
- ❑ Abstracts
- ❑ Full text
- ❑ Mark records
- ❑ Display records
- ❑ Print records
- ❑ Save records to disk
- ❑ E-mail records

Familiar with/competent in all of the above for:
- ❑ Library catalog (Web version)
- ❑ Library catalog (text version)

Figure 10.3 *Continued*

Figure 10–3. *Continued*

- ❑ FirstSearch databases
- ❑ ABI/Inform Business Periodicals on Disc
- ❑ General Periodicals on Disc
- ❑ PubMed

LIBRARY CATALOG
- ❑ Search by Author
- ❑ Search by Title
- ❑ Search by Subject
- ❑ Search by Keyword
- ❑ Search by Call Number
- ❑ Identify locations and item status (non-circ, on shelf, checked out, bindery)
- ❑ Print from catalog
- ❑ When to refer questions to reference librarians

Installing a New Toner Cartridge in the Computer-Lab Printer

1. If you find that the printer's "Toner Low" light is on or that print-outs are coming out faint or streaked, open the printer door labeled "**Door A**," remove the toner cartridge, and shake it from side to side about five or six times. This normally gets another 50 to 100 pages of printing out of the toner cartridge.

2. If the cartridge has already been shaken or shaking does not solve the problem, get a fresh toner cartridge from the Reference Office supply closet. Be sure to get cartridge model number A1520.

3. Remove the fresh cartridge from its packaging and install it according to the instructions that come with it. Be sure to remove the orange tab and shake the cartridge from side to side five or six times after removing the tab.

4. Put the old cartridge in the box the fresh cartridge came in and return it to the Reference Office supply closet. Attach a yellow sticky note to the box and write on the note the word *Used* and the date and time the cartridge was replaced.

FAQs

A FAQ (Frequently Asked Questions) format is good for describing something that is not linear enough to fit neatly into a list format. A FAQ also has the advantage of being a familiar format for anyone who has used the Web. Writing a good FAQ requires you to anticipate questions staff will have and to write clear, compact answers to those questions. Seeking input from staff while developing a FAQ is a must.

Pay To Print FAQ

Public-access computer users must pay to print in the library's computer labs. The following questions and answers should help you assist users who wish to print.

Q: **What is the cost for printing?**
A: Seven cents per page.

Q: **How can users pay for printing?**
A: The same debit card that is used to pay for photocopies can also be used to pay for printing. Users can purchase a new debit card, or add value to an old one, at vending machines on the 1st and 3rd floors. Users cannot pay for printing with bills or coins.

Q: **Once users send print jobs, can they cancel them without being charged?**
A: Yes. At any point up to the moment they insert their debit cards into the card reader attached to the printer, users can cancel print jobs without being charged.

Q: **Can staff delete print jobs?**
A: Yes. Every print job is held in a cue and can be deleted from the cue any time before it is printed. Each print job must be given a name by the user before it is sent, making it easy to distinguish between print jobs. Jobs that are not printed within 24 hours of being sent to the printer are automatically deleted.

Q: **What if the printer malfunctions in the middle of a print job?**
A: Normally, once the malfunction is fixed, the printer will reprint any lost or misprinted pages and then print the rest of the print job. If users lose print pages they have paid for due to a printer malfunction, staff can use the debit card kept at the lab service desk to reprint the job without additional charge to the user.

Tutorials

Tutorials are a sophisticated form of self-study training material that walks trainees step-by-step through a complex task or set of tasks. Tutorials that require trainees to answer questions or solve problems as they go along can be evaluated by trainers to identify any gaps in the trainee's knowledge. Tutorials are a lot of work to develop and maintain, so you need to be sure any tutorial you create will actually be useful and will be used. You may find that some staff resent doing tutorials, perhaps because bad tutorials smack of busywork. The following is an example of a tutorial:

Staff Tutorial for Searching RanganCat	**Page 2 of 12**

SEARCHING BY AUTHOR

An author is any individual (personal author) or organization (corporate author) that has written, edited, illustrated, composed, or otherwise had significant creative input on a book or other intellectual property.

In RanganCat, search personal authors by typing last name first, followed by first name or first initial. If you type only the last name, you get *every* author with that last name. You can also include the author's middle name or initial if you know it. One you have typed in the information, click Author to perform the search.

Example: Personal Author

SEARCH: | williams t |

AUTHOR   TITLE   SUBJECT   KEYWORD   CALL NUMBER

Search corporate authors by typing in the name of the organization in its normal order and then clicking Author to perform the search.

Example: Corporate Author

SEARCH: | world health organization |

AUTHOR   TITLE   SUBJECT   KEYWORD   CALL NUMBER

Exercise

Search each of the following authors and enter the number of hits (items in the catalog) that are retrieved for each author.

Author	Number of Hits
terry williams	_____
s. e. hinton	_____
united states department of energy	_____
chicago public library	_____

What is the title of one item in RanganCat written by Wallace Stegner?

_____

Call number? _____   What floor is it on? _____

Tutorials can be taken to another level if they are made interactive by being mounted on a Website. Properly designed, Web-based interactive tutorials allow trainees to seamlessly practice what they are learning as they work their way through the tutorial. Through the use of forms, trainees can even submit their answers electronically. Of course developing and maintaining such tutorials involves considerable work, so you must decide if the payoff will be worth the effort.

Audio/video training

The notion of interactive tutorials brings up the whole issue of using audio/video media for training purposes. Audio/video is best used for delivering training needed by a large number of staff at different times. An orientation for new staff is one example of training that lends itself well to audio/video formats. Before jumping onto the audio/video bandwagon be aware that such training is expensive and time consuming to produce. Also keep in mind that trainees (especially those of the MTV generation) may not respond well to audio/video training materials that reflect low production values.

Videotape

There are some convincing reasons not to use videotape for training. A first-class training video is both time consuming and expensive to develop—a professionally produced ten-minute videotape can easily cost several thousand dollars. If you choose to develop a professional-quality training video, take into account the cost of production, the number of staff who will potentially see the video, and the fact that most training videos have disappointingly brief useful lives. Even if professional-quality training videos are beyond your means, the idea of capturing live training on tape for repeated use later on is still tempting. One inexpensive possibility is to videotape classroom-type training sessions so that those who cannot attend can watch the video later. This is done most simply by mounting a video camera on a tripod, pointing it toward the front of the room, and letting the tape roll. Somewhat better is to have a volunteer camera operator to track the trainer and zoom when appropriate. The problem with videotaping training sessions is that it can be an inducement for staff not to attend the live training. "I'll just watch the video later," is a promise often made but rarely kept. Also keep in mind that videotaping a computer screen or a projected computer screen produces disappointing results.

Audiotape

Audiotape training materials are cheaper to produce than the videotape variety, though they too suffer from a short useful life. Producing a simple audiotape requires nothing more than a tape recorder, though the results will be significantly better if you use professional sound equipment and employ the services of a trained narrator. Audiotape can be used by itself or in conjunction with printed materials and is most often used to create guided tours of facilities. If you are thinking of developing an audiotour, treat yourself to a museum audiotour or two. You can learn a lot by paying attention to the techniques museum audiotours use to guide visitors and maintain interest.

Slide shows

The 35-millimeter slide show and its cousin, the filmstrip, are both expensive to develop and update. Much more feasible are slide shows developed with computer software such as Harvard Graphics or Microsoft PowerPoint. With a bit of practice, anyone can create slide shows that incorporate text, photographs, images, sound, and even video clips. Once created, such slide shows are easy to update. Staff can view and listen to slide shows at any workstation equipped with a sound card and speakers or headphones.

INSTRUCTOR-PROVIDED TRAINING

As stated above, self-study materials cannot entirely replace the need for the kind of interactive instruction that can be provided through face-to-face human contact.

One-on-one training

One-on-one training can be the most effective type of training because it is the most interactive. Because it is also the most labor-intensive type of training, one-on-one training needs to be done selectively, possibly as a follow-up to self-study or group training. If one-on-one training is the best way to introduce some particular skill, the burden of providing training can be reduced by creating a "training tree." Say, for example, all computer-lab staff must learn how to eradicate the Have A Nice Day virus which keeps reappearing on lab computers and you decided that one-on-one training is the best way to teach this skill. You, as primary trainer, work one-on-one to train three staff on how to eradicate the virus. Each of these staff members are then assigned three trainees whom they train one-on-one. These trainees then become trainers who are assigned trainees, and so on until everyone on the staff has been given one-on-one training. This not only lightens the training load, but it is also a good way to get one-on-one training to staff whose regular work hours do not overlap with work hours of the primary trainer but do overlap with those of secondary or tertiary trainers. The downsides are that training can get distorted as it is passed down the training tree (accompanying written materials can help eliminate this problem) and that some trainers may fail to follow through on their assignment to train others.

Focus On:

Training Users, Training Staff

Can the same materials be used both to train staff and to educate users? This is a worthwhile question to ask, since employing a single store of materials for both purposes is an efficient use of resources. Staff and users are not the same, of course. Because staff are selected through a hiring process that selects (or should select) for certain desirable qualities or skills, even inexperienced staff are assumed to have more knowledge than users. Staff training materials thus make assumptions about staff that are not true for most users; also, staff training materials may provide information (such as passwords) that should not be made available to users. On the other side of the coin, materials for educating users may either be too basic for staff or fail to provide staff with all the information they need to do their jobs.

Nonetheless, there is likely to be a lot of shared ground between staff training and user education. Wise managers will take advantage of this to save themselves time and trouble. For example, if the user-education department has a well-developed new-student orientation, it does no harm for new staff to sit through it even if it does cover some things they already know. Another example might be requiring new staff work through a user-education tutorial on searching online databases. While such a tutorial might not teach new staff everything they need to know about online databases, it is a good starting point from which to build even greater knowledge. Similarly, there may be staff-training materials that can be of benefit to users, though these generally need to be adapted so that they do not assume too much starting knowledge and do not include information that users do not need (or should not be permitted) to know.

Group training

Group training is less interactive than one-on-one training, but it is also less labor intensive. Small-group training that involves only a few trainees can often be conducted on the spot, while gathered around a public-access workstation or at the service desk. Larger groups are generally trained in a classroom setting. Because it is difficult and costly to bring together a large number of staff for a training session, it is important that group training be effective. Covering everything that goes into effective group training would fill a much larger book than this. There are some key points that any trainer should know:

Do not cover too much

Most trainers try to cover too much in too short a time. In staff training, five main points in an hour is about the limit. Well-prepared trainers pick their main points ahead of time and decide on the best way to teach each point. It is a good idea to provide trainees with an outline of main points to be covered and to stick to the outline during the training session.

Keep training interactive

No training session should be a non-stop monologue by the trainer, and trainers need to rid themselves of the notion that just because they "covered" something does not mean that the trainees actually learned the topic. Trainees need time to absorb and practice what is being taught. There must also be time for questions and answers. A common training mistake is to ask, "Any questions?" and then rush onward without allowing even a few seconds for trainees to formulate and ask questions. If you ask for questions, silently count to five (at least) before moving on. Remember, too, that different people learn in different ways. Trainers should provide a mixture of learning methods to accommodate different learning styles: lecture, demonstration, written hand outs, and hands-on practice should be part of all group-training sessions.

Use active-learning techniques

The best way to make training interactive is to use the techniques of active learning. These techniques range from brain storming to role playing to hands-on practice. One good source for active-learning techniques is *Designs for Active Learning: A Sourcebook of Classroom Strategies for Information Education.*[2] Hands-on learning is by far the best way to teach computer skills, and the best setting for computer training is one where each student has a workstation on which to practice what they are learning. Teaching computer skills without hands-on computers is about as effective as teaching cross-country skiing without snow.

Tip Sheet

Inducements to Attend Training

One of the most frustrating experiences for a manager is to arrange a training session only to see half of those who said they would attend turn into no-shows. (Of course it is always the half that most needs the training and/or complains the loudest about not getting enough training that does not show up.) You can try to improve attendance by making training *mandatory*, but what does this really mean? Are you willing and able to sanction staff who miss *mandatory* training? What will you do when Jack, the tenured cataloger who cheerfully puts in four hours a week at the computer-lab service desk, cannot make it to a training session? When your best work-study student begs out of training to study for a big physics exam? Chances are, there is nothing you can do in such situations. There are, however, steps you can take to induce staff to attend training and/or complete self-study materials.

SALARY

While it is unlikely that you have any control over the salary of regular staff, you may have some salary flexibility when it comes to work-study students or lower-level clerical staff. For example, you might hire new work-study students at one pay level with the promise of a small raise in their per-hour rate once they have completed a prescribed course of training. This course of training might include such elements as completing a training checklist, completing a set of tutorials, or attending a certain number of staff-training sessions.

EVALUATIONS

Though you might not write formal evaluations on everyone who works with public-access computers, you should make it a point to mention training in the evaluations of those staff you do evaluate. You should also mention training if you have occasion to report to supervisors of those staff who put in hours in your area but do not report directly to you.

BRIBES

If you put several hours into preparing a training session, spending a few dollars on coffee and donuts (or some other treat) is a small price to pay if it improves attendance. Offering a small door prize can also improve attendance. As silly as it may seem, any door prize that you can arrange— a book bag or poster picked up at a conference, a hour of comp time, a coupon for a free book at the next library book sale—can be an effective incentive. The chance to earn an extra hour or two of pay is also an incentive, so part-time staff who are paid on an hourly basis (such as work-study students) should be paid for attending training sessions, even if the session is not held during their regularly scheduled hours.

GOOD TIMING

Always arrange training for times when the most staff can attend. Surveying staff to find out the best times for them may be helpful, but past experience is probably the surest guide. It may be that, in your organization, late Wednesday afternoon is a good time. Or maybe late Friday morning works best. Times such as Monday mornings, Friday afternoons, finals week, and the days leading up to or following major holidays are notoriously bad for training. You may find that you need to offer a training session on more than one day and time to accommodate everyone; be sure, though, that you do not offer the same training so many times that you draw only a few attendees to each session. If you have regular staff meetings that are well attended, you might make a short training session part of each meeting or occasionally devote an entire meeting to training.

GUEST TRAINERS

If the same person always leads every training session, things are bound to get a little stale. Inviting various members of the staff to conduct training sessions will spice things up a bit as well as involve additional staff in the training process. Inviting in a trainer from outside your department (such as someone from the systems department) or from outside the library (such as someone from the campus information technology office) will also provide variety.

ADVERTISING

Even in a small organization, it pays to advertise training sessions. Send out an announcement (via e-mail or on a paper flyer) far enough in advance so that staff can adjust their schedules to attend. Two weeks advance notice should be enough in most cases. It is a good idea to ask people to RSVP to such announcements, though do not count on everyone who says they will come actually showing up for the training. The day before the training session, send out a reminder via e-mail or voicemail.

PROVIDE GOOD TRAINING

The best way to get staff to attend training sessions is to get a reputation for providing good training. If the training you provide is either ineffective or does not train staff in the areas where they want and need training, attendance will remain low.

NOTES

1. See *Yahoo!*: BBSs (*dir.yahoo.com/Computers_and_Internet/Communications_ and_Networking/BBSs/Software*).
2. Gradowski, Gail, Loanne Snavely, and Paula Dempsey. 1998. *Designs for Active Learning: A Sourcebook of Classroom Strategies for Information Education*. Chicago: Association of College and Research Libraries.

11 USER RELATIONS

The management of public-access computers can be represented as a triangle. At the base of the triangle are hardware and software, the essential stuff that must be in place for public-access computers to exist at all. One leg of the triangle represents the staff necessary to keep public-access computers up and running and to assist the public in using those computers. This chapter will focus the third leg of the triangle, user relations. User relations includes communicating with users, getting feedback from users, and dealing with conflicts that involve users.

COMMUNICATING WITH USERS

To provide good public service, you need to communicate to users the following information about your library's public-access computers:

- Who can use the computers.
- When and where they can be used.
- What software applications, databases, and other electronic resources are available.
- How to use those software applications, databases, and other electronic resources.
- Rules and policies governing computer use.
- Changes involving any of the above.

Communicating some of the above information, such as when and where public-access computers can be used, is easy. Communicating other information, such as how to use software applications, is a full-time, never-ending job.

There are a few basic rules for communicating with users that you should always follow:

Focus On:

Acceptable-Use Policies

One way in which libraries communicate with their users is through written acceptable-use policies. In general, such policies codify:

- Who can use public-access computers.

- What can and cannot be done on public-access computers.

- What happens to those who violate the acceptable-use policy.

The specifics touched upon by acceptable-use documents can range from hardcore systems issues—*Users may not download files to workstation hard drives*—to issues that range into the realm of basic freedoms—*Users may not view Websites that espouse hate or which advocate violence*. Acceptable-use policies can easily become politically charged documents, so it is necessary that the contents of any such policy be thought through with great care and with input from people both within and outside of the organization. The more people involved in creating an acceptable-use policy, and the more varied their backgrounds and orientations, the more likely that the final policy will be fair and workable.

What exactly goes into an acceptable-use policy will vary from one place to the next, but once an acceptable-use policy has been written and approved it must be made available to the public though library bulletin boards, newsletters, and Web pages. After all, if library users do not know what is in an acceptable-use policy it is impossible for them either to abide by or to seek changes to it.

- Communications should be on the user's level. Just as you should avoid technical and library jargon when communicating with users, also avoid talking down to users.
- Keep communications as short as possible. Do not bog down users with extraneous details, prolonged explanations, or any unessential information.
- Try to communicate essential information through more than one medium. For example, essential information might be communicated through printed handouts, a newsletter, the library Website, *and* signage.

- Neatness, clear layout, correct spelling, and proper grammar all contribute to the credibility of written communications. Thoroughly edit and proofread any written communication intended for public consumption. Use multiple editors and proofreaders to catch mistakes and to make sure that all instructions are clear.
- Mass communications that reach many users are more cost effective than one-on-one communication. This does not mean that you should abandon one-on-one communication with users, rather that you should use mass communication whenever possible.

SIGNAGE

Signage can be an effective means of communication, but only if it is used well. For examples of good signage, pay attention to the signage you see in hospitals, airports, and grocery stores. Two key signage mistakes that you will rarely see in places that use signage well are 1) too many signs and 2) signs used for purposes to which they are not well suited.

Too many signs

Have you ever seen a political discussion degenerate into a shouting match? At the point where everyone starts shouting at once, there is a great deal of noise but nobody really hears anything. The same thing happens when there are too many signs: overburdened with visual clutter, the human brain actually starts blocking out visual images.[1] To prevent visual clutter, you must keep the number of signs to an absolute minimum. Similarly, you need to keep wording on signs as brief as possible.

Things that signs are not good at

Signs are not good at explaining complex processes that involve multiple choices. They are not good at explaining abstract concepts. They are not good at deterring thieves, vandals, or hackers. And, by themselves, signs are not good at stopping well-intentioned people from doing things that seem perfectly reasonable to them. A sign that reads:

> **Do Not Insert Disks
> in Computer Drives**

will not, all by itself, stop people from inserting disks in computer drives. You could, though, use such a sign in conjunction with drive locks or security software as part of a program to stop users from putting disks in disk drives.

What are signs good for?

They are good for identifying things:

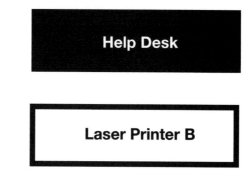

Strategically placed, signs are good for giving physical directions:

Signs are good for stating matters of fact:

Signs are good for giving brief, uncomplicated instructions:

When you start asking signs to do more than the things described above, you are asking too much of them.

Signs should look neat and professional. Scrawled, handwritten signs send a bad message. Even temporary out-of-order signs should be printed out, not handwritten. Small signs can be printed in-house on regular paper or, for a better look, on cardstock. Be sure to use a clear, readable font: Arial (a sans-serif font) and Times New Roman (a serif font) are safe, conservative choices. Be sure to leave some negative space around the text of any sign.

Little negative space makes text harder to read:

More negative space makes text easier to read:

Backing paper signs with poster board and covering them with clear plastic laminate helps preserve a neat appearance, but any sign must be replaced once it starts to look ragged or dirty. The text of signs should be kept short. Make sure several people look over drafts of signs for clarity and correctness.

Point-of-use signs

Point-of-use signs are typically small signs placed where a specific activity is conducted. The sign below, if attached to a workstation monitor, would be an example of a typical point-of-use sign:

> **This workstation prints
> to Laser Printer B**

Point-of-use signs can be used to give step-by-step instructions, but only if the number of steps are few and the instructions themselves are simple. The type size of the text on any point-of-use sign must be large enough to be read clearly from the distance users will be when they encounter the sign. Do not overuse point-of-use signs: plastering a single workstation or work area with multiple point-of-use signs creates visual clutter, causing the signs to all but disappear. Sticky-tape Velcro is a good way to attach point-of-use signs to monitors, printers, and the like. Molded clear-plastic sign stands are good for displaying 8.5" × 11" inch signs on desktops. Taping signs to desktops is useless, as the signs will be covered with books, papers, and backpacks without being read.

Display signs

Display signs are typically hung from walls or ceilings, though they can be supported by easels. The type size of display signs must be large enough to be read from a distance. For example, the letters on signs suspended from a typical library ceiling should be at least three inches high. Permanent display signs are best manufactured by professional sign makers. Before going to the considerable expense of acquiring permanent display signs, it is a good idea to have a local sign shop make temporary display signs on foam core. These temporary signs are relatively cheap, look good, and last long enough to let you decide where you want your permanent signs to go and what, exactly, you want them to say.

Electronic signage

Unlike traditional signs, electronic signs have the advantage of being easy to change. They may also incorporate such attention-grabbing features as animation, video, and sound.

Though some types of electronic signage, such as video kiosks that incorporate touch-screen technology, are quite expensive, it is possible to use a spare microcomputer and presentation software (such as Microsoft PowerPoint) to develop inexpensive electronic signage in-house. Begin by using the presentation software to create a series of slides containing information you wish to communicate to users. One slide might give the computer lab's hours. Another might list the major software applications available in the lab. Another might say "No food or drink near computers." Remember, if you use too many slides no one will have the endurance to stand there long enough to watch them all roll past. Once you've created the presentation, it can then be loaded onto a microcomputer (an older machine will do) and, along with a monitor, placed on a desktop or computer stand. You can even suspend the monitor from the ceiling if you use a mounting bracket and an extension monitor cable. Whether on a desktop or suspended from the ceiling, a large monitor works best. If noise is not a problem, you can incorporate sound into the slide presentation as long as the computer you are using has a sound card and speakers. Use the timing and loop features of the presentation software to set the presentation to loop continuously. When you set the timing, allow each slide enough time so that users can read it before the program moves on to the next slide. Once the timing is set and the presentation is looping (continuously repeating), remove the keyboard and mouse to prevent anyone from stopping or altering the presentation. The presentation can be updated or completely redone at any time.

A rock-bottom type of electronic signage can be created using the screen-saver feature found on Windows 95/98 computers. To turn screen savers into electronic signage:

1. Choose **Start, Settings, Control Panel.**
2. Double click the **Display icon** from the **Control Panel.**
3. Click the **Screen Saver** tab.
4. From the **Screen Saver** menu choose **Scrolling Marquee.**
5. Click **Settings.** In the text box, type a brief message such as, "One-hour time limit in effect 8–5 M–F."
6. If you wish, you can select the font, adjust type size, change text and background colors, select a scroll speed, and set the number of minutes that must pass before the screen saver appears.

PUBLICATIONS FOR USERS

Along with signage, print publications can be used to communicate with users. Essentially everything that was said about publications in Chapter 9, "Staffing Issues," holds true for publications aimed at users. User-oriented newsletters, tip sheets, lists of instructions, FAQs, Web-based publications, tutorials, and so on, can be used to inform and instruct users just as they are used with staff. The difference, of course, is the audience, so when developing user publications you will need to strike a balance between soaring over the heads of your audience and talking down to them. Even more so than with staff publications, drafts of user publications need to be read by others (including, ideally, actual users) who can give feedback. The week after you have printed out 12,000 copies of a user guide is not the time to find out that the instructions it contains are far too technical for the average person.

GROUP TRAINING FOR USERS

In many libraries, user education is the responsibility of someone other than the manager of the public-access computers. In such cases, it is important that you keep those responsible for user education current on any changes affecting the public-access computers and that you regularly suggest areas in which users need training. If, for example, you report that users do not know how to print from public-access workstations, instructors can incorporate the necessary training into user-education sessions; without any input, the instructors might not even know that printing is a problem for users. Along the same lines, it is a very good thing if everyone in user education works at least an hour or two a week at the public-access computer-service desk so they can experience for themselves what users know, and do not know, about using computers.

If, as manager of the public-access computers, the job of training users falls to you, then you have a full-time job indeed. Developing, scheduling, advertising, and teaching classes on all but the smallest scale is a huge undertaking. Without extraordinary staff resources to call on, you will have to be selective about what you teach and how often you teach it. As with publications, most of what is said about group training in Chapter 9, "Staffing Issues," is true of group training for users, though user training is, of course, aimed at a different audience.

FEEDBACK FROM USERS

Feedback from users is one of the ways you learn whether or not users are satisfied with public-access computer resources and services. For this reason, feedback should be one factor in deciding what resources and services you provide. There are two types of feedback. One is the unsolicited feedback that users offer up on their own. The other is feedback gathered in systematic ways in order to obtain valid information about users' wants and needs.

UNSOLICITED FEEDBACK

Most unsolicited feedback comes in the form of complaints or compliments. Though these seem like direct opposites, they share some common characteristics. For one thing, it is easier to hear the complaints and compliments you want to hear than it is to hear those you would rather not hear. If, for example, you are an advocate for allowing the use of e-mail on public-access computers, it is only natural that comments like, "We can do our e-mail here? Great!" ring louder in your ears—and register more permanently in your memory—than the complaints of users who feel computers should be used for research only. Another shared characteristic of both complaints and compliments is that they tend to represent extremes. Thus, while some vocal users may be strongly in favor of e-mail, and other vocal users may be strongly opposed to it, it is quite possible that the silent majority of users do not care one way or the other. Finally, the complaints and compliments of users who are either VIPs (Very Important Persons) or VSPs (Very Strident Persons) are often heard more clearly than the complaints and comments of others. If the president of the university were to say to the library dean, "I walked through your computer lab yesterday and the garbage on the screens looked like it belonged in an adult bookstore, not a library," would it carry more weight than a similar complaint made by an undergraduate? If an angry user were to go screaming to the branch manager with threats to sue for discrimination because he cannot check his e-mail, would it carry more weight then the comments of a polite user who says, calmly and sincerely, that she would like very much to be able to check her e-mail in the library? The answer to both questions is, in almost every case, "Yes."

The point of bringing up the similarities between complaints and compliments is this: making policy decisions solely or largely on the basis of either complaints or compliments is a serious mistake. Other factors—including the library's mission statement, long-standing library policies, user input that has been gathered in systematic ways, staff input, and practical experience—must be considered along with complaints and compliments if you wish to make wise and fair decisions.

HANDLING COMPLAINTS

One of the least-pleasant aspects of managing public-access computers is handling user complaints. There are, however, a few techniques you can use to make the process as painless and productive as possible:

Listen

Start by letting the person with a complaint state their case with little or no interruption from you. Nod your head, look attentively at the other person, and act interested even if you have heard this same complaint many times before.

Repeat what the other person says

Starting with a phrase like "Let me see if I understand this...," restate in your own words your understanding of what the other person said. If the other person agrees that you understand the situation, you can say something like, "I sympathize with your frustration" (which is not the same thing as saying you think their complaint is justified).

Explain the library's position

While it should not be your purpose to win a debate with the other person, as an employee of the library it is your job to explain the library's position—even if you do not happen to agree with it 100 percent. (See below for some strategies for explaining.)

Make promises carefully

Make a promise only if you are absolutely sure you can keep it. "I'll bring up your complaint the next time I meet with my department head" is an example of a promise you can and should keep. Never make promises you cannot keep and avoid making promises in the heat of the moment.

Admit the other person is right (when appropriate)

Sometimes complaints are justified, and there is nothing wrong with admitting the other person is right. In some cases, such admissions may lead to change: "You've got a good point. I'm going to suggest to the director that we set one-hour time limits on workstations instead of half-hour limits." Sometimes, though, you will be able to offer little more than sympathy: "Yes, it is ridiculous that we only have ten workstations, but there is no way we are going to be able to add more this fiscal year. I have already asked for more workstations from next year's budget."

Offer alternatives

Alternatives that may seem obvious to you are not necessarily obvious to your users, so offering an alternative or two is always a good idea.

- "I understand that paying for printing is a hardship for a student, but do you know that you can download as much information as you want to diskette free of charge?"
- "Yes, the workstations are often full, but do you know you can reserve a two-hour block of workstation time up to two days in advance?"

Know when to quit

Discussions can reach the point where they become pointless. At such times, it is necessary to break off and send the complaint up the organizational ladder. "I hear what you are saying, but I can't give you what you want. I will be happy to help you schedule an appointment to speak with...(my supervisor, the library director, the chair of the library board, etc.). Similarly, your staff should know to refer any serious complaint to you rather than get embroiled in a debate with a user.

Close on a positive note

If you have not done so already, wind up by asking the person with the complaint for ideas on how to improve the situation. Write down any ideas the other person offers and promise to discuss them with staff and management. Be sure to thank the other person for their feedback and to take down the information you need to contact them later.

EXPLAINING THE LIBRARY'S POSITION

Here are some techniques you can use to explain the library's position to those with complaints:

Facts

Sometimes simply stating the facts is enough to satisfy a complainant. A statement of fact such as, "We charge for printing from computers because if we didn't we would have to spend $25,000 a year on paper and toner," can be sufficiently convincing.

Analogies

Analogies are useful for showing how computer policies are in line with traditional library policies: "Computer workstations are like books. The library makes books available, but we do not guarantee that the book you want will not be checked out or otherwise in use when you come to the library. In the same way, we provide access to computer workstations, but we can not guarantee that there will be one available for you every time you walk into the library."

Mission and policy statements

Mission statements and policy statements can be used to show how a library practice or policy conforms to the library's mission. "Our mission statement says that the library's primary role is to 'support teaching and research at the university,' and that is why university students, staff, and faculty have priority over visitors when it comes to using the library's computers."

User demand

If the library has made efforts to systematically gather input from users, the data can be used to justify a policy: "We did a user survey last fall, and 71 percent of our users said they thought being able to use e-mail in the library was essential."

Explaining the needs of other users

Sometimes users complain about a policy without understanding that other users have different needs than they do. "I understand that students using library computers for word processing ties up the computers, but not every student on campus has a word processor at home like you do. There are those who really appreciate the fact that they can use library computers to write their research papers."

If it is important to control you anger in feedback situations, it is just as important to control your enthusiasm for making everyone happy. When dealing with complaints, sometimes no action is the best course of action. If you try to make everyone happy by taking action on every complaint, you will soon find that complaints are like the mythological Hydra: cut off one head, and two more spring up in its place; make one person happy by acting on a complaint, and two other people jump up to complain about the action you have just taken.

Tip Sheet

Thou Shall Not Get Mad

No matter how rude, impossible, or just plain crazy a complainer may be, do not get mad. Keeping your cool is not always easy, of course, but when you feel your jaw setting, your throat getting tight, or your blood pressure climbing, there are some techniques you can use to keep the situation from escalating.

- Do not assume that everyone who complains is angry. It is a lot easier to keep your own emotions in check if you go in thinking, "This person genuinely wants to make this a better library," rather than, "Oh my gosh, this jerk is really angry." Focus on the content of the feedback, not the interpersonal dynamics of the situation.

- Even if you feel angry, try not to let it show. Control the level and tone of your voice. Try to sound more like Mr. Rogers and less like Mr. T. Avoid gestures and body postures that can be perceived as angry: do not wave your hands or clench your fists; lean back in your chair rather than forward; nod your head while the other person speaks to show that you are listening; keep a comfortable distance between yourself and the other person.

- If either you or the other person's anger seems to be escalating out of control, find an excuse (or make up a lie, if necessary) for a short cooling-off period: "I'm scheduled to meet with the library director right now. Can you give me a couple of minutes to run upstairs and reschedule?" or "Can we discuss this in my office instead of here in the lab? I'll meet you there just as soon as I find someone to take my place at the desk." Spend the cooling-off period taking deep breaths, splashing water on your face, venting to a trusted colleague—doing whatever you can to get a little distance on the situation and keep your anger under control. Do be careful not to leave the other person alone so long that their anger builds or they simply give up and walk out.

Unless you want to head for early career burn out, you must accept the fact that there will always be complaints and that you are never going to please everyone. Remember, too, that acting too hastily on a complaint, even when done out of the desire to provide outstanding service, almost always leads to a bad decision. Before acting on any complaint, take time to think it through, discuss it with others, and consider all your options.

WRITTEN FEEDBACK FORMS

Formal feedback (not complaint) forms are a valuable tool, especially when the library takes them seriously and makes a point of showing users that they take them seriously.

- Feedback forms should be available at every service point and via the Web.
- Feedback forms should have spaces for users to write their names and contact information.
- Feedback forms should provide users with information on where/ how to submit a completed form.
- Once a feedback form has been submitted, the library should have a procedure in place to make sure that someone from the library responds on the telephone or in writing (e-mail or paper).
- The person from the library who responds should be someone who is knowledgeable about the matter or matters the user feedback touched upon.
- User feedback (with user's names and contact information removed), along with the library's written response, can be displayed on a prominent bulletin board.
- All written comments from users should be categorized and archived for later reference.
- Comments submitted via the Web should be treated in the same way as comments written on paper.

Figure 11–1. Sample Feedback Form

**RANGANATHAN LIBRARY
ELECTRONIC RESEARCH CENTER**

Feedback Form

Please tell us what you think. If you include your name and phone or e-mail, we will make a personal reply.

Name: _____

Phone: _____ E-mail: _____

Date: _____

I use the Electronic Research Center (ERC):
- ○ More than once a week.
- ○ Several times per month.
- ○ Less than once a month.
- ○ First time I've used ERC.

The service I received today was:
- ○ Very helpful.
- ○ Somewhat helpful.
- ○ Not very helpful.
- ○ Not at all helpful.

In general, I find that the hardware and software resources in the ERC meet my research needs:
- ○ Always. ○ Most of the time. ○ Some of the time. ○ Never.

COMMENTS:

Thank you for your feedback. Drop completed forms at Circulation Desk or mail to address on the opposite side of this form. Send feedback via the World Wide Web at: *www.ranganathanlib.org*.

SYSTEMATICALLY GATHERED FEEDBACK

Gathering user feedback in a systematic way can help you get a sense of how a true cross section (as opposed to a vocal minority) of users feel about the public-access computing resources and services in the library. The trick to getting meaningful information from systematically gathered feedback is to develop and administer a valid user survey.

USER SURVEYS

The library literature is filled with articles reporting on "user surveys," "satisfaction surveys," and the like. Even though only some of these articles are about public-access computers, reading through a few of them can give you a good sense of how to design and administer a valid survey. The ARL SPEC kit "User Surveys in ARL Libraries," provides many examples of user surveys conducted in libraries.[2] If you are truly serious about conducting a valid user survey, and especially if you are interested in publishing your results, then you should consult with someone who is an expert on research design and surveys (such as a statistician).

One crucial element of a user survey is the wording of the questions. If the questions in a survey are either leading or unclear, they will produce bad data. A lot of eyes (some of them belonging to people from outside the library) should look over your questions before you use them. Piloting questions on users before conducting the actual survey is a must.

A second crucial element of a user survey is finding a way to come up with a true random sampling of users to question. There are many ways to do this. You could choose names at random from your database of cardholders. Or you might choose to survey every third person who walks into the computer lab during certain periods of time. A completely different approach might be to contact people who do not use public-access computers to find out why. However you select the sample of users to question, be aware that the selection method will shape your findings.

Most likely, your research design will call for surveying individual users either in person or via telephone. Another approach is to use a focus group composed of users selected to be representative of your entire user base. For example, in a university setting a focus group might be composed of faculty members, laboratory researchers, graduate students, undergraduate students, and local high-school students. The members of the focus group are brought together and asked questions designed to elicit their thoughts on resources and service. A focus group requires as much or more work and pre-planning than traditional users surveys, and a focus group works best when a skilled, impartial moderator is brought in from outside to run it.

LIMITATIONS OF FEEDBACK

The great limitation of user feedback is that users can only tell you what they want based on what they know. For example, a user might tell you she is very happy with the public-access computer services in the library, but this satisfaction may be based on ignorance of what services could be offered. By the same token, a user might say he is very unhappy with public-access computer resources without any knowledge of how those resources compare with resources provided by similar libraries. So, while feedback can be enlightening, and while systematically gathered feedback is preferable to unsolicited random feedback, feedback should not be your only guide when making decisions about computer resources and services.

CONFLICTS WITH USERS

Libraries that provide public-access computers have different interests than the users they serve. For example, it might be in a user's interest to access every feature a public-access computer could possibly provide. On the other hand, the library's interest in preserving the integrity of public-access computers will likely cause the library to deny access to certain features on its computers. From such opposing interests, conflict inevitably grows. Because conflict is inevitable, the best that managers of public-access computers can do is manage conflict so that, though present, it does not come to dominate the relationship between the library and its users.

FAIRNESS

Perhaps the best way to keep conflicts manageable is to treat users fairly. Even when users disagree with a library practice or policy, users who feel they have been treated fairly are much less likely to feel angry about the situation than those who feel unfairly treated.

One important element of fairness is giving users a fair hearing when they have complaints or suggestions. Anyone who feels they have been listened to fairly and openly is likely to feel less hostile than someone who feels shut out. The above paragraphs on dealing with user feedback offer suggestions on how to give users the opportunity to be heard.

Another aspect of fairness is treating all users equally in terms of access to resources and the amount of help they receive from staff. A written policy on providing help to users (see Chapter 9, "Staffing Issues") is one tool for ensuring fair treatment. Conveying to staff the importance of treating everyone fairly, of not playing favorites, and (above all) of not discriminating against users on the basis of race, creed, national origin, and so on, should be a part of both initial and ongoing training. Everyone has users they like working with just as everyone has users they do not like working with, but personal feelings need to be set aside in the library. The only time users should receive unequal treatment is when it is called for in library policies, as is the case with policies that call for different levels of access/assistance for adults as opposed to children, or for cardholders as opposed to non-cardholders.

Of course some might argue that providing extra assistance to users with disabilities is unequal treatment, but the counter argument is that the extras provided to users with disabilities are intended only to level the playing field with non-disabled users. After all, the Americans with Disabilities Act calls for "reasonable accommodation," not "unfair advantage."

Consistency

A close cousin to fairness, consistency is also important for making users feel they are being treated fairly. For example, if there is a no-food-or-drink policy in the computer lab, then the policy should be enforced at all times, and, as much as possible, enforced in the same way by each member of the staff. If a policy is enforced Monday through Friday, it should be enforced on weekends as well. If drinks in closed sports bottles are allowed by some of the staff, then they should be allowed by all staff. If users cannot have a cup of coffee in the computer lab, then staff cannot have one either.

The key problem with inconsistent enforcement of rules is that it is terribly unsettling to users. Imagine the feelings of a user who has used the computer lab five times and, each time, visited a favorite Web chat room without any problem. Then, on his sixth visit, a staff member growls at him as if he has just committed a major felony. To make matters worse, on his next visit to the computer lab the user looks around and sees staff totally ignoring the fact that half the people in the lab are visiting Web chat rooms. Such inconsistent enforcement of rules cannot help but put users on edge and can introduce an element of anarchy to the atmosphere of the public-access computer facilities.

Finally, it is important to note that consistency also embraces the idea that treatment of users needs to be the same from one person to the next. If staff helps User A access HotMail, they cannot turn around and refuse to help User B do the same thing. Such favoritism is frustrating to users and, in the worse cases, can lead to formal discrimination complaints.

Rationing Access

In most public-access computer settings, the biggest problem is that there is more demand for workstations than there is supply. In some ways, this is a good problem; one stemming from the popularity of the resources offered. Still, it is a never-ending source of complaints and conflicts. The ultimate solution to the problem is more workstations, though there is always the argument that, realistically, no amount of workstations will ever be enough.

CONTROLLING WHAT USERS CAN DO

One approach to making sure there are enough workstations to go around is to limit what users can do on workstations. This can be done by simply not providing certain types of software. For example, if the main purpose of workstations is conducting research, then not providing productivity software prevents the workstations from being used for word processing or creating slide-show presentations. Another way in which workstation activities can be controlled is to use filtering software or proxy-server technology to block out Websites that offer such unscholarly diversions as games, chat, and e-mail. In addition, or alternatively, staff can be assigned the duty of shooing users off of forbidden Websites, though this practice is labor intensive, stressful, and prone to inconsistency.

Controlling what users do on workstations is controversial because, critics say, it can hinder intellectual freedom. After all, one person's frivolous waste of time and resources can be another person's serious intellectual pursuit. Worse, this type of control can result in absurd situations, such as one in which User A is not allowed to check her e-mail for a message containing a citation to a journal article she needs while User B is allowed to spend two hours looking at Websites devoted to his favorite movie star.

SETTING TIME LIMITS

A different approach is to set time limits on workstation use. A single user might be limited, for example, to two one-hour time slots per day. Time limits can be enforced automatically by software programs or through some type of paper-and-pencil sign-up system overseen by staff. One paper-and-pencil system involves putting sign-up sheets on clipboards mounted next to each workstation. The sign-up sheets spell out the rules for signing up and have time slots in which users can write their names. Such a system can be nearly self regulating, as users at the workstation can see if someone has signed up to use the workstation after them, and those who have signed up usually let the person at the workstation know when time is up. Figure 11–2 shows an example of a workstation sign-up sheet.

Figure 11–2. Sample Sign-up Sheet

Workstation Sign-up Sheet

Workstation # _____   Week of _____

THE RULES

- One user may sign up for no more than two (2) one-hour time slots per day.
- Anyone who is more than 10 minutes late will lose their time slot.
- You may continue using a workstation if others are not waiting.
- The sign-up system is in effect from 10:00 A.M. to 8:00 P.M., Monday–Friday only.
- You can reserve time slots in person or by calling 208–555–1212.

Time	Monday	Tuesday	Wednesday	Thursday	Friday
10:00–11:00 AM					
11–Noon					
Noon–1:00 PM					
1:00–2:00 PM					
2:00–3:00 PM					
3:00–4:00 PM					
4:00–5:00 PM					
5:00–6:00 PM					
6:00–7:00 PM					
7:00–8:00 PM					

Some libraries use their online public-access catalog as a way to set time limits on public-access workstations. First, each workstation is cataloged much like a book and a loan period (30 minutes, one hour, etc.) is set. Users then check out workstations with their library cards and can be issued fines if they use the workstation beyond its loan period. This practice is described in Karen G. Schneider's "So They Won't Hate the Wait: Time Control for Workstations," an article which provides a fine overview of the entire topic of time limits on public-access workstations.[3]

There are a number of commercial software packages that allow system administrators to set time limits on workstations. For a comparison of these products, see Jack Albrecht's Computer Timers: Specs and Evaluations (*home.earthlink.net/~coyote8/timers.htm*).

Time limits are normally enforced only when others are waiting to use workstations. Allowing users to sign up in advance, either at the service desk or via telephone, makes a time-limits system popular with those who want to be assured access to a workstation on a specific day and time. It is not necessary to use the time-limit strategy with every workstation, as establishing time limits on just a handful of workstations may be sufficient. A few express workstations with very short (15- to 30-minute) time limits may do the trick as well.

USER CATEGORIES

A third way to ration access to public-access workstations is to create user categories and give some categories more access privileges than others. For example, in a university setting the students, faculty, and staff of the university might have priority access over those not affiliated with the university; or, in the extreme, those not affiliated with the university might be denied access altogether. In a public library, cardholders might have priority access over non-cardholders; or adult cardholders might have priority access over children; or child cardholders might be allowed access only in the children's room. The permutations and combinations of user categories and the privileges the various categories are allowed are endless and entirely dependent on local situations and institutional missions. As a tool for rationing access, user categories are likely to please those who find themselves in the privileged categories while, at the same time, alienating those in the less- or un-privileged categories. In addition, user categories will not improve the access situation if, even after some users have been declared more privileged than others, there are still not enough workstations to satisfy demand.

PROBLEM USERS

Many people in the library profession do not like to use the term *problem user* because the term is overly negative and reductionist. After all, sometimes the fault lies more with a *problem library* than with a problem user. Acknowledging that the term is not perfect, it still applies to some users. Problem users are a concern for managers of public-access computers because there is something about computers that seems especially attractive to this type of user. Perhaps it is the subversive aura of the Internet and hacking culture. Perhaps the high demand for public-access computers brings out the worst competitive behaviors in users, prompting them to take undue advantage of the resources and of their fellow users.

Whatever it is that attracts them to public-access computers, a few problem users can make life unbearable for staff as well as for other users. Problem users may routinely monopolize more than their fair share of computer and staff resources. They may lodge non-stop complaints, harbor unreasonable expectations, make unreasonable demands, bully staff and other users, or constantly push the limits of acceptable behavior. They may annoy staff and other users in ways ranging from routinely butting in where they are not wanted to smelling bad because they never wash. So long as problem users do not violate the law, there may be little or nothing you can do about them. Those "We reserve the right to refuse service to anyone" signs seen in restaurants are not an option in libraries open to the public.

Suppose, for example, you have one user who makes a habit of going around the computer lab completely turning down the screen brightness on every workstation that is not in use. This odd habit does not really hurt anything, but it is an annoyance to staff and users. The first rule when dealing with this type of behavior is not to overreact or act prematurely. You do not want to make a federal case out of some minor annoyance that might simply go away if left to run its course. Remember that patience very often wins out in cases of this type. Your first active step when dealing with a minor problem should be to talk to the person who is causing the problem. Be sure to explain why the behavior is a problem and ask the user to stop. Sometimes reason prevails. Sometimes the person stares back at you and mutters something like, "I have to do it. The light from all the screens blocks out my voices." If a problem of this sort persists, you could write a policy that addresses the specific problem, but it is almost always a bad idea to make policy based on the actions of one or two atypical users. When you make a policy, you must be prepared to enforce it equally on everyone; otherwise, it is not policy, it is discrimination. If a minor problem continues or escalates, it should be brought to the attention of senior library administrators and library legal counsel. There may be legal steps your institution can take, but they should be taken by those who know the law for a living, not by amateurs.

UNACCEPTABLE BEHAVIOR

While it is wise to be patient with merely annoying behavior, behavior that crosses the line into the territory of the unacceptable should not be tolerated:

Criminal acts

Typical criminals acts committed in computer areas include theft, vandalism, destructive computer hacking, indecent exposure, touching oneself or someone else in a sexual way, and viewing child pornography. Call the police whenever anyone commits a blatantly illegal act in the presence of you, your staff, or other users, but do not put anyone in danger in an attempt to stop a crime. It is better to let a thief walk out the door with a computer than to get anyone (including yourself) hurt.

Threats

There is a world of difference between a user who issues a threat along the lines of "I'm going to sue you for discrimination" or "I'm going to get you fired," and a user who threatens violence. The latter type of threat is a police matter that must be taken absolutely seriously. Not everyone who threatens to harm someone follows through on their threat, but such persons are many times more likely to act violently than is someone who has never uttered a threat.

Stalking

Any type of stalking behavior—following, unwanted or inappropriate attentions, inappropriate telephone calls—is a red flag. In many states, stalking is crime, and even where it is not a crime it is possible to get a restraining order. If you supervise young employees, such as student workers, be aware that young people often fail to recognize stalking behavior or else dismiss it as harmless: "Oh, he's just flirting with me." If you see a user's behavior toward anyone on your staff escalating to stalking behavior, you should speak to the staff member about it and discuss their options with them. By the same token, staff should not in any way stalk or thrust unwanted attentions on users.

Harassment

Harassment is not part of anyone's job description and is unacceptable behavior in users and staff alike. Whether or not particular behavior constitutes harassment is sometimes a tough call. If someone on your staff feels they are being harassed by a user, of if you feel that one of your staff is being harassed, you should turn to your institution's sexual harassment policy and/or the office in your institution that handles harassment complaints.

WHEN TO BECOME CONCERNED ABOUT USER BEHAVIOR

While most user misbehavior falls into the category of "Annoying But Harmless," it is important to keep in mind that annoying behavior can escalate towards more serious behavior. As a general rule, trust your instincts and those of your staff. If a user's behavior scares or upsets you or members of your staff, there is probably something to those feelings and you should contact senior library administration and the police. Contacting the police is important because they may be able to tell you if the person in question has been a problem in the past. Past behavior is the best predictor of future behavior, so if you learn from the police, or though any other means, that a user whose behavior concerns you has committed a violent act in the past, it is time to seek help from whatever authority can best insure the safety of all concerned. Behaviors to be genuinely concerned about include:

- Contact with staff outside the library, including phone calls at home.
- Inappropriate or excessive attention directed at a particular staff member or user.
- Inappropriate comments—especially those of a sexual or threatening nature.
- Inappropriate loitering.
- Inappropriate attention-getting behavior such as obsessively asking for help from a particular staff member or purposely breaking minor rules so as to get attention from staff.
- Going out of the way to expose someone else to Web pages with sexually explicit or violent images, or printing out such images and deliberately leaving them where others will see them.

NOTES

1. Kastner, Sabine, Peter De Weered, Robert Desimone, and Leslie G. Ungerleider. 1998. "Mechanisms of Directed Attention in the Human Extrastriate Cortex As Revealed By Functional MRI. *Science*. 5386 (October): 108–111.
2. Brekke, Elaine. 1994. User Surveys in ARL Libraries: A SPEC Kit. Washington, D.C.: Association of Research Libraries, Office of Management Services.
3. Schneider, Karen G. 1998. "So They Won't Hate the Wait: Time Control for Workstations." *American Libraries*. 11 (December): 64–65. (*www.ala.org/alonline/netlib/il1298.html*).

INDEX

V

vandalism, 121
VDT placement, 27
Vendaprint, 99
VGA, 50
video cameras, 53
video cards, 54
video display terminals (VDTs), 30, 49–50
videographic accelerators, 54
videotape training, 184
violence, 64
voice mail, 163
volunteers, 141

W

WAN, 9, 10
warranties, 56
water pipes, 121–122
Web, 14–16
    browsers, 14, 67–68
    browsers, security, 136

    cameras, 121
    communicating with staff, 167–169
    pages, 14
    servers, 8, 9–10
Web4Lib, 55, 105, 124
wide area networks, 9, 10
Windows NT, 8, 128
Windows Policy Editor, 128
WINSelect KIOSK, 125, 136
Wintel, 4, 47
WinU, 63, 125
word processors, 61, 67
workstations, modular, 19
workstations, placement, 31–33
World Wide Web *see* Web
written communication, 163–169
WRQ Express, 64
WS_FTP, 15
WWW *see* Web

Z

Z39.50, 15–16
Zip disks, 50–51, 131

ABOUT THE AUTHOR

Donald A. Barclay is currently the assistant director for the Health Informatics Education Center at the Houston Academy of Medicine—Texas Medical Center Library in Houston, Texas. A 1990 graduate of the School of Library and Information Science at the University of California at Berkeley, in the past he has held professional library positions at the University of Houston and New Mexico State University. In addition to publishing in library science, he has published in the fields of children's literature and the literature of the American West. He lives on Galveston Island, Texas, with his wife, Darcie.